PENGUIN PLAYS

WESKER: VOLUME TWO

ARNOLD WESKER (F.R.S.L., Litt.D.), born in Stepney in 1932, was taught at Upton House School in Hackney. His education came mainly from reading books and listening to BBC Radio. From 1948 to 1958 he pursued many trades from furniture maker to pastry cook. His career as a playwright began when Lindsay Anderson, who had read *The Kitchen* and *Chicken Soup with Barley*, brought Wesker to the attention of George Devine at the Royal Court Theatre; Devine, uncertain about *Chicken Soup with Barley*, sent it to the Belgrade Theatre in Coventry, where it was first produced in 1958 under the direction of John Dexter. A year later, having been turned down by the Royal Court, *Roots* was directed by Dexter, again at the Belgrade, Coventry, and in the following months he directed *The Kitchen* at the Court for two Sunday night experimental performances 'without decor'. Later in 1959 *I'm Talking about Jerusalem* was added to make up *The Wesker Trilogy*, which created an enormous impact when produced in its entirety at the Royal Court in 1960 and again at the Shaw Theatre in 1978. In 1979 the National Film Development Board commissioned a film script of the three plays, which, because Wesker made many cuts and additions, is a new work – *The Trilogy* twenty years on! Over 350,000 copies of the Penguin edition have been sold, and the hardback is in its fifth printing.

His other plays are *Chips with Everything* (1962, voted 'Play of the Year'), *Their Very Own and Golden City* (1965; winner of the Italian Premio Marzotto Drama Award in 1964), *The Four Seasons* (1965), *The Friends* (1970), *The Old Ones* (1972), *The Journalists* (1972), *The Wedding Feast* (1974), *Shylock* (1975, previously entitled *The Merchant*), *Love Letters on Blue Paper* (1977), *One More Ride on the Merry Go Round* (1978), *Caritas* (1980), *Annie Wobbler* (1981), *Four Portraits – of Mothers* (1982), *Yardsale* (1984), *Whatever Happened to Betty Lemon?* (1986), *The Mistress* (1988); these last five form the cycle of *One-Woman Plays*; *Bluey* (1984, European Radio Commission), *Sullied Hand* (1985), *When God Wanted a Son* (1986), *Badenheim 1939* (1987, adapted from the novel by Aharon Oppelfeld), *Shoeshine and Little Old Lady* (1987, a series of one-act plays for young people), *Lady Othello* (1987), *Beorhtel's Hill* (1988, community play commissioned for the 40th anniversary of Basildon) and *The Mistress* (1988).

In addition to plays for the stage Arnold Wesker has written television and film scripts, poems, short stories and numerous essays, and lectures. He has published two collections of essays, *Fears of Fragmentation* (1970) and *Distinctions* (1985), and three volumes of stories, *Six Sundays in January* (1971), *Love Letters on Blue Paper* (1974) and *Said the Old Man to the Young Man* (1978). In 1974 he wrote the text for a book of primitive paintings of the East End by John Allin, *Say Goodbye You May Never See Them Again*. In 1977, after a brief stay in the offices of *The Sunday Times* to gather material for *The Journalists*, he published an account of his visit called *Journey into Journalism*. In 1978 came *Fatlips*, a book for young people, and in 1988 he wrote a libretto for an opera of *Caritas*, with music by Robert Saxton. Penguin have published six volumes of his plays and a collection of short stories under the title *Love Letters on Blue Paper*.

From 1961 to 1970 Arnold Wesker was artistic director of Centre 42, a cultural movement for popularizing the arts primarily through trade-union support and participation. From 1981 to 1983 he was President of the International Playwrights' Committee. He is a grandfather and lives with his wife and one of his three children in North London.

ARNOLD WESKER

Volume 2

The Kitchen/The Four Seasons/
Their Very Own and Golden City

PENGUIN BOOKS

PENGUIN BOOKS

Published by the Penguin Group
27 Wrights Lane, London W8 5TZ, England
Viking Penguin Inc., 40 West 23rd Street, New York, New York 10010, USA
Penguin Books Australia Ltd, Ringwood, Victoria, Australia
Penguin Books Canada Ltd, 2801 John Street, Markham, Ontario, Canada L3R 1B4
Penguin Books (NZ) Ltd, 182–190 Wairau Road, Auckland 10, New Zealand

Penguin Books Ltd, Registered Offices: Harmondsworth, Middlesex, England

The Kitchen
First published by Penguin Books 1960
Fuller edition, revised by Arnold Wesker, published by Jonathan Cape 1961
Published by Penguin Books in *Three Plays* (Schaffer, Wesker, Kops), 1968
Copyright © Arnold Wesker, 1960, 1961

The Four Seasons
First published by Jonathan Cape 1966
Published in Penguin Books 1966
Reprinted with revisions 1990
Copyright © Arnold Wesker, 1966, 1990

Their Very Own and Golden City
First published by Jonathan Cape 1966
Published in Penguin Books 1967
Copyright © Arnold Wesker, 1966, 1981

This collection published in Penguin Books 1976
Reprinted with revisions 1981, 1990
3 5 7 9 10 8 6 4 2

All performing rights of *The Kitchen*, *The Four Seasons* and *Their Very Own and Golden City* are fully protected, and permission to perform any of the plays, whether by amateurs or professionals, must be obtained in advance from Ian Amos, Duncan Heath Associates, 162–170, Wardour Street, London W1V 3AT

Made and printed in Great Britain by
Richard Clay Ltd, Bungay, Suffolk

CONTENTS

The Kitchen

A PLAY IN TWO PARTS
WITH AN
INTERLUDE

The original, shorter version was first presented by the English Stage Society at the Royal Court Theatre on 13 September 1959. This full-length version was first presented by the English Stage Company at the Royal Court Theatre on 27 June 1961, with the following cast:

MAGI	Tommy Eytle
MAX	Martin Boddey
BERTHA	Jessie Robins
MOLLY	Jane Merrow
WINNIE	Ida Goldapple
MANGOLIS	Marcos Markou
PAUL	Harry Landis
RAYMOND	Andre Bolton
HETTIE	Rita Tushingham
VIOLET	Alison Bayley
ANNE	Gladys Dawson
GWEN	Jeanne Watts
DAPHNE	Shirley Cameron
CYNTHIA	Sandra Caron
DIMITRI	Dimitri Andreas
BETTY	Tarn Bassett
JACKIE	Charlotte Selwyn
HANS	Wolf Parr
MONIQUE	Mary Peach
ALFREDO	Reginald Green
MICHAEL	James Bolam
GASTON	Andreas Markos
KEVIN	Brian Phelan
NICHOLAS	Andreas Lysandrou
PETER	Robert Stephens
FRANK	Ken Parry
CHEF	Arnold Yarrow
HEAD WAITER	Charles Workman
MARANGO	Andreas Malendrinos
TRAMP	Patrick O'Connell

Directed by John Dexter

INTRODUCTION
AND NOTES FOR THE PRODUCER

The lengthy explanations I am forced to make may be annoying; I am sorry, but they are necessary.

This is a play about a large kitchen in a restaurant called the Tivoli. All kitchens, especially during service, go insane. There is the rush, there are the petty quarrels, grumbles, false prides, and snobbery. Kitchen staff instinctively hate dining-room staff, and all of them hate the customer. He is the personal enemy. The world might have been a stage for Shakespeare but to me it is a kitchen, where people come and go and cannot stay long enough to understand each other, and friendships, loves and enmities are forgotten as quickly as they are made.

The quality of the food here is not so important as the speed with which it is served. Each person has his own particular job. We glance in upon him, highlighting as it were the individual. But though we may watch just one or a group of people, the rest of the kitchen staff does not. They work on.

So, because activity must continue while the main action is played out, we shall study, together with a diagram of the kitchen, who comes in and what they do.

The waitresses spend the morning working in the dining-room before they eat their lunch. But throughout the morning there are about three or four who wander in and out carrying glasses from the glassery to the dining-room and performing duties which are mentioned in the course of the play. During the service the waitresses are continually coming out of the dining-room and ordering dishes from the cooks. The dishes are served on silver and the waitresses take about six plates out of the hot-plate immediately under the serving-counter. Stocks of plates are replenished all the time by the porters. These are highly efficient waitresses. They make a circuit round the kitchen calling at the stations they require. They move fast and carry large quantities of dishes in their arms.

The kitchen porters, who are a mixture of Cypriots and Maltese, are divided into various sections. Firstly there are those who do the actual washing of cutlery, tins and plates by machine; these we do not see. For our purpose we only use one porter, who continually replaces clean plates under the serving-counter so that the waitresses can take them as required. He also sweeps up at regular intervals and throws sawdust around.

The woman who serves the cheeses and desserts and coffee, we hardly and rarely see through the glass partition back of stage, but every now and then she comes to the pastry-section to replenish her supplies of tarts and pastries.

Now to the cook. At this point it must be understood that at no time is food ever used. To cook and serve food is of course just not practical. Therefore the waitresses will carry empty dishes, and the cooks will mime their cooking. Cooks being the main characters in this play, I shall sketch them and their activity here, so that while the main action of the play is continuing they shall always have something to do.

NOTE

The section dealing with the service starting on p. 39 with 'Two veal cutlets' is the actual production worked out by John Dexter based on what was originally only an indicative framework set out by me. I wish to acknowledge his creation of this workable pattern.

The pattern of service falls into three stages of increasing speed. (1) From 'Two veal cutlets,' p. 39, to Gaston's 'Max send up steaks and mutton chops quick,' p. 41, the pace is brisk but slow. (2) From then on to Peter's cry of 'Too old, too old my sweetheart,' p. 43, the pace increases. (3) From then on to the end of the part, 'Have you all gone barking-raving-bloody-mad,' the pace is fast and hectic.

If trouble is taken to work out this pattern then the right rhythm will be found.

Any producer is at liberty to abstract this set if he can still convey the atmosphere.

CHARACTER SKETCHES IN ORDER OF STATIONS

FRANK, Second Chef, *Poultry*: A prisoner of war for four years. Now at thirty-eight he has an easygoing nature. Nothing really upsets him, but then nothing excites him either. He drinks steadily throughout the day and by nightfall is blissfully drunk though instinctively capable. Flirts with the waitresses, squeezing their breasts and pinching their bottoms.

ALFREDO, *Roast*: An old chef, about sixty-five and flat-footed. Large-muscled and strong, though of medium height. He is a typical cook in that he will help nobody and will accept no help: nor will he impart his knowledge. He is the fastest worker there and sets-to straight away, not stopping till his station is all ready. He speaks little, but he has a dry sense of humour. He is the worker and the boss is the boss, and he probably despises the boss. He hums to himself as he works.

HANS, *Fry*: A German boy, nineteen, pimply and adolescent. He is working in London through a system of exchange. He speaks very bad English and is impressed by anything flashy. Yet as a German he is sensitive.

PETER, *Boiled Fish*: Peter is the main character. Another young German, aged twenty-three, who has worked at the Tivoli for the last three years. His parents were killed in the war. He is boisterous, aggressive, too merry, and yet good-natured. After three years at the Tivoli one might say he was living on his nerves. He speaks good English but with an accent, and when he is talking to people he tends to speak into their ear as though he were telling them a secret. It is a nervous movement. A strong characteristic of Peter is his laugh. It is a forced laugh, pronounced 'Hya hya hya,' instead of 'ha ha ha'. He turns this laugh into one of surprise or mockery, derision or simple merriment. There is also a song he sings – music at p. 14 – which ends in exactly the same laughter. Somehow its maniacal tone is part of the whole atmosphere of the kitchen.

KEVIN, *Fried Fish*: The new young man, Irish, twenty-two. He spends most of his time being disturbed by the mad rush of the work and people around him. This is worse than anything he has ever seen.

GASTON, *Grill*: A Cypriot by birth, forty-odd, slight and dark-complexioned. Everyone-is-his-friend until he starts work, then he is inclined to go to pieces and panic and cry at everyone. When the play starts he has a long scratch down the side of his face.

MICHAEL, *Eggs*: There is nothing particular about this boy of eighteen. He is what his dialogue will make him; but he is a cook and before long all cooks are infused with a kind of madness.

BERTHA, *Vegetable Cook*: Large woman, coarse, friendly, narrow-minded, Jewish.

MANGOLIS, *Kitchen Porter*: Young Cypriot boy, cheeky, hard-working, dashing in and out of fast-moving kitchen, replenishing plates on hot-plate.

ANNE, *Dessert and Coffee*: Irish, soft-spoken, thirty-five, easy-going. Speaks with slow, cloying lilt.

MAX, *Butcher*: A stout man of fifty. Loud-mouthed, smutty and anti anything that it is easy to be anti about. He has a cigarette continually drooping from his mouth, and like Frank drinks steadily all day till he is drunk.

NICHOLAS, *Cold Buffet*: Nicholas is a young Cypriot who has lived in England three years and can therefore speak reasonable English but with an accent. Speaking the language and working in a capacity socially superior to his compatriots, who are dishwashers, he behaves with a wild heartiness, as one who is accepted. And as one who is accepted he imitates, and he chooses to imitate Frank and Max by becoming drunk by the end of the day.

RAYMOND and PAUL, *Pastrycooks*: Paul is a young Jew; Raymond is an Italian who speaks almost perfect English but with an accent. These two pastrycooks, as opposed to the madmen in the kitchen, are calm and less prone to panic. The rush of the kitchen does not affect them; they work hard and straight through without the afternoon break but have no direct contact with the waitresses. Raymond is emotional. Paul is suave, though not unpleasant.

CHEF: A large man of about fifty-nine with tiny moustache. If he could, he would work elsewhere – preferably not in the catering trade at all. The less that is brought to his attention, the happier he feels. In such a large kitchen the organization carries itself almost automatically. He rarely speaks to anyone except Frank the second chef, Max, who works near him, and Nicholas, who is immediately under him. He will not say good-morning nor communicate any of the politeness expected of a chef. Familiarity, for him, breeds the contempt it deserves.

MR MARANGO, *Proprietor*: An old man of seventy-five, stout – but not fat – with flabby jowls and a sad expression on his face. A magnificent curtain of grey hair skirts the back of his bald head and curls under itself. His sad look is really one of self-pity. The machine he has set in motion is his whole life and he suspects that everyone is conspiring to stop it.

THE ACTIONS

For the purpose of the action of this play, the following dishes have been allotted to the following cooks. Of course they cannot go through all the actions necessary for the cooking of these dishes. The two important things are:

1. That they have some actions to mime throughout the play in between speaking their parts and gossiping among themselves, and
2. That by the time the service is ready to begin they have an assortment of neatly arranged trays and pots of 'dishes and sauces' ready to serve to the waitresses as requested.

FRANK: Roast pheasant/chips. Roast chicken/pommes sautés. Mushrooms. Pour salt in twenty chicken carcasses, place in oven. Slice carrots and onions and boil for gravy. Salt and place pheasants in oven. (Both carcasses are cleaned elsewhere.) Chop mushrooms and fry together with sauté.

ALFREDO: Roast veal/spaghetti. Boiled ham/boiled potatoes. Roast beef for staff. Season and cook veal and beef in oven. Boil spaghetti in salt water. Chop onions and carrots and make sauce. Place ham in pot to boil.

HANS: Sausages/baked rice. Pork chops/white beans. Vegetables for the staff. Cut up ham, tomatoes, onions and mushrooms, and sauté for rice. Boil white beans. Pork chops are fried during service. Collect from cold cupboard and heat yesterday's vegetables for staff.

PETER: Mixed fish/sauce. Cod meunière/boiled potatoes. Boiled turbot/sauce hollandaise. Beat egg yellows on slow heat, add melted margarine for sauce hollandaise. This takes a long time. Slice cod and turbot into portions. Slice lemons for garniture.

KEVIN: Grilled sardines/boiled potatoes. Grilled salmon/boiled potatoes. Fried plaice/chips or boiled potatoes. Slice lemons for plaice. Cut salmon into portions. Arrange four trays on bench: one for oil, one for milk, one for flour, and one with required fish. Clean grill with wire brush.

GASTON: Grilled chops/chips. Grilled steak/chips. Most of his work is done during service. Clean grill with wire brush. Collect from vegetable-room and then blanch chips. Aid Kevin.

MICHAEL: Hamburger/eggs on top/chips. Ham omelet. Onion soup. Cut ham for omelet. Cube stale bread for onion soup. Crack eggs in tin ready for omelet. We assume enough soup left over from yesterday.

MAX: Mainly carting of huge meat carcasses from cold-room to bench where he then proceeds to cut and dissect them.

NICHOLAS: Cold roast beef/potato salad. Cold ham/Russian salad. Slice meats and arrange various trays of salad. Also roll and slice in portions chipped meat for Michael's hamburgers.

CHEF: Mainly clerical and organizational work of course. He will mind his own business as much as possible.

PAUL and RAYMOND: Bands of apple and pear tart. Pastry called 'Religieuse'. First bake trays of tarts prepared day before. Spread custard sauce and then slice fruit to lay on top. Make more pastry; mix flour and fat, add water, roll out. Cut into more bands ready for tomorrow. Fill pastry with cream from cloth bag. Peel fruit.

BERTHA: Assume all her vegetables, sprouts, cabbage, spinach and sauté, were cooked day before. She merely has to heat them over. Otherwise gossips with coffee woman.

PETER'S SONG

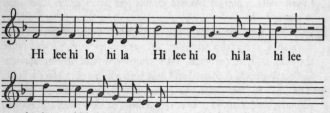

Hi lee hi lo hi la   Hi lee hi lo   hi la   hi lee

hi lo   hi la ha ha ha ha ha   *continue down the scale in laughter*
hya hya hya hya.

PART ONE

There is no curtain in this part. The kitchen is always there. It is semi-darkness. Nothing happens until the audience is quite seated (at the appointed time for commencement, that is).

The night porter, MAGI, *enters. He stretches, looks at his watch, and then stands still, realizing where he is. It is seven in the morning. Then with a taper he lights the ovens. Into the first shoots a flame. There is smoke, flame, and soon the oven settles into a steady burn, and with it comes its hum. It is the hum of the kitchen, a small roar. It is a noise that will stay with us to the end. As he lights each oven, the noise grows from a small to a loud ferocious roar. There will be this continuous battle between the dialogue and the noise of the ovens. The Producer must work out his own balance.*

As MAGI *lights the fourth oven,* MAX *enters, goes straight to the lower cold cupboard and collects a bottle of beer, which he opens and starts to drink. As* MAGI *lights the last oven,* BERTHA *enters to her station. As she passes* MAX *she says,* 'Good-morning, Max.' *He burps.*

BERTHA: Here, Magi, give us a hand with this.

MAGI: O.K., love.

BERTHA: There.

    [*Enter* MANGOLIS.]

MAGI: Bertha – that ten shillings.

BERTHA: You haven't got it? So you haven't got it! You going away?

MAGI: No.

BERTHA: Then I'll wait.

MAGI: You're a good girl, Bertha.

BERTHA: Good – I am; but a girl – unfortunately not

MAGI: Go on, *I* could fancy you.

BERTHA: Me? Boy, I'd crack you in one crush. Crrrrrunch!

MAX: Magi, give us a hand please.

MAGI: Bertha – you worry me.

BERTHA: I worry him.

    [MAX *and* MAGI *raise the beef on to* ALFREDO's *oven. As they do this,* BETTY *and* WINNIE, *waitresses, enter, mumbling, and go through to the dining-room.* PAUL *and* RAYMOND *enter with their tools under their arms. They go to their own corner.* MAGI *exits.*]

PAUL [*to anybody*]: Good morning, good morning. [*To* BERTHA] Good morning, me old darling. [*To* MAX] And to you too, Max.

MAX [*his soul not yet returned*]: Good morning.

BERTHA: Morning.

RAYMOND: Max, it's escalope of veal on today?

MAX: How many?

RAYMOND: Three. I'll take them now and put them in my box, before the others get there.

[MAX *goes to cold-room, and returns with three escalopes which he slaps down on his table and* RAYMOND *collects.* MANGOLIS *delivers empty dustbins to their places.*]

MAX: And don't forget my puff pastry tomorrow.

RAYMOND: Usual?

MAX: Usual.

PAUL [*to* RAYMOND *as he returns*]: It's Religieuse today?

RAYMOND: Yes. But you do the fruit bands, leave the pastries, I'll do them. Motor bike working all right?

[HETTIE *and* VIOLET, *waitresses, pass through to the dining-room.*]

HETTIE: This is the way to the dining-room.

VIOLET: I'm not used to working in places like this, I used to be at the old Carlton Tower.

PAUL: Bloody thing! No more second-hand gear for me.

RAYMOND: What is it?

PAUL: If I knew it wouldn't be so bad. Mechanical contraptions! It takes me all my time to find out where the alarm on a clock is.

RAYMOND: I'll look at it.

PAUL: You know about motor bikes?

RAYMOND: In the war I was a dispatch rider – I had to know.

PAUL: I left it at home though.

RAYMOND: I'll come to your home then.

PAUL: I'll make you a supper.

RAYMOND: We'll have an evening of bachelors.

PAUL: A bachelors' evening.

RAYMOND: A bachelors' evening. We'll use the veal cutlets Max promised.

PAUL: Good idea. What about your wife?

RAYMOND: Sometimes it's a good thing to miss a wife.

PAUL: Yes.

RAYMOND: I'm sorry, I forgot.

PAUL: Don't worry on my account – she was a fool. If she'd only been a bitch it wouldn't have mattered but she was a fool as well.

RAYMOND: It's not such a big hurt then?

[*Enter* ANNE *to her station.*]

PAUL: For me? No! But she's going to have children one day and those kids are going to have a fool for a mother – that's what hurts.

RAYMOND: You don't miss her?

PAUL: I don't miss her. Good morning, Anne. [*She doesn't hear.*] Good morning, Anne.

ANNE: Good morning, boys.

PAUL: That's better.

RAYMOND: Good morning, sweetheart.

ANNE: Hello boys, hello Max.

MAX [*his soul returned*]: Top o' the mornin' to you Anne.

ANNE [*putting coffee in metal jug to warm on oven*]: An' the rest o' the day to yersel', dear. [*Stretching herself.*] Ah, me bed was lovely.

RAYMOND [*lasciviously*]: I bet it was.

ANNE: Hey, Raymond, tell me, what happened to Peter in the end, you know, last night?

RAYMOND: Now he's a silly boy, eh? Don't you think so? I don't even know what it was all about anyway. You know, Paul?

PAUL: All I know is he had a fight with Gaston. Why? I don't know. Over a ladle I think, or maybe a . . .

MAX: He's a bloody German, a fool, that's what he is. He is always quarrelling, always. There's no one he hasn't quarrelled with, am I right? No one! That's some scheme that is, exchanging cooks! What do we want to exchange cooks for? Three years he's been here, three years! [*Exits to get more beer.*]

ANNE: Ah, the boy's in love.

RAYMOND: What love! You ever see him? When Monique does a turn as hostess by the stairs he watches her through that mirror there. [*Points to glass partition.*]

ANNE: Rubbish.

RAYMOND: And he walks round the kitchen and looks to see if she's talking or flirting with any of the customers.

ANNE: I don't believe it.

BERTHA: Never.

RAYMOND: You don't believe me?

PAUL: And they quarrel in front of everybody as well. They shout at each other. Shout! You know, sometimes she doesn't even look at him, and waits for her orders with her back turned.

ANNE: The poor boy. He's no parents you know. But what happened last night? I want to know.

   [MAGI *re-enters*.]

MAX: Ask Magi.

MAGI: Any coffee, Anne?

ANNE: Sure dear. (*Pours*.) Help yourself.

RAYMOND: Hey Magi, what happened with Peter last night, uh?

MAGI [*unconcerned*]: They nearly killed him.

ANNE: Oh God.

RAYMOND [*gesticulating*]: But what was it all about, tell me? I don't know nothing, me.

MAGI: Well *you* should know that – I wasn't here.

PAUL: All we know is that they suddenly started shouting at each other. And you know, Peter always shouts more than the other and you can always hear Peter – well, so then it stopped, and then a few seconds later they were fighting, and I saw Gaston raise a boning knife and Peter knock it out of his hand, and then . . .

RAYMOND: And then he lifted him and nearly sat him on the stove and . . .

PAUL: And then the Chef came along and . . .

ANNE: Well, I saw the Chef separate them and I heard Gaston say 'I haven't finished yet, it's not over yet,' but I still don't know what it was all about.

PAUL: Who cares? I say good morning to Peter but never good night.

MAGI: Well I came in at nine last night. The boys were changing and suddenly Peter comes and Gaston follows him. Gaston says Peter called him a lousy Cypro and the boys make circle round him and want to murder him! All of them . . . but Peter says 'No, everyone for me is the same – it makes no difference race, you misunderstand . . .' They all wanted to hit him! And he was scared! I never seen him so white.

ANNE: But what was it about to begin with?

MAX: A ladle, I tell you.

PAUL: Who knows? There's always fights, who knows how they begin?

MAGI [*laying down cup*]: Well, I'm going.

PAUL: Have a good kip, old son.

ANNE: And I must get started too. [*Looks round empty kitchen.*] You wouldn't think this place will become a madhouse in two hours, would you now. [*Moves off with* MAGI.]

   [RAYMOND, PAUL *and* MAX *continue to work in silence. Enter* DAPHNE, GWEN *and* CYNTHIA, *waitresses, to dining-room.*]

DAPHNE: So if he doesn't come home tonight I'm going to leave.

CYNTHIA: Well he does have to work in the afternoon.

GWEN: That's right.

MAX: Any luck on the pools, Ray?

RAYMOND: Huh!

MAX: Norwich and Leyton let me down. Twenty points. Twenty points!

   [*Enter* HETTIE *from dining-room for a coffee. Pause.*]

HETTIE: Morning, Annie love.

PAUL: Read about the man in the mental home who won thirty-five thousand pounds?

RAYMOND: And his wife turned up after eighteen years?

   [*Enter* DAPHNE *from dining-room for a coffee.*]

PAUL: Eighteen years!

   [*Pause.* DIMITRI *enters. A Cypriot kitchen porter, young, good-looking and intelligent. He is carrying in his hand a home-made portable radio. He is happy as he takes it to* PAUL. *He speaks with an accent.*

   Enter MOLLY, JACKIE, *waitresses, to dining-room.*]

DIMITRI: I make it Paul, I make it. There! [*Lays it on table near by.*] She does not look handsome. I'm sorry for that.

PAUL: Ah you good boy, Dimitri. Can we play it? [*He looks round to see if authority is in sight. Only* DAPHNE *and* HETTIE *approach. One has a bucket in her hand and her hair is tied up with a scarf. The other is similarly attired and carries a feather duster.*] Anyone around?

HETTIE [*pointing to portable*]: What is it, Paul?

PAUL: Is Marango around yet?

DAPHNE: Not yet. Whose is it?

PAUL: It's mine. Dimitri here made it.

19

RAYMOND: You made it on your own? All those little wires and plugs? Tell me, what are you doing here? Why you waste your time with dishes in this place? You can't get a job in a factory?

DIMITRI: A factory? You think I find happiness in a factory? What I make there? Uh? This little wire, you see it? This I would make, or that ... what you call it?

PAUL: Knob.

DIMITRI: Knob. That perhaps I could put in. All day I would fix knobs. I tell you, in a factory a man makes a little piece till he becomes a little piece you know what I mean?

RAYMOND: Hey Dimitri, *you* know what happened to Peter last night?

DIMITRI: They nearly kill him.

DAPHNE: Oh my Gawd.

DIMITRI: But you think it was all Peter's fault? They all wanted to fight. Listen, you put a man in the plate-room all day he's got dishes to make clean, and stinking bins to take away, and floors to sweep, what else there is for him to do – he want to fight. He got to show he is a man some way. So – blame him!

[DIMITRI *turns on the radio, which plays a loud rock 'n' roll tune.* PAUL *grabs* DAPHNE, *and starts to dance,* HETTIE *tries to dance with* DIMITRI, *who won't* ... HANS *enters, grabs* HETTIE, *they dance. At the height of the dance,* MONIQUE *enters from the dining-room.*]

MONIQUE: Marango's in the dining-room.

ALL: What!

MONIQUE: Marango's in the dining-room.

[*There is a scramble to restore everything to normal, work is resumed,* DIMITRI *vanishes into the plate-room with the radio.* HANS *exits. Enter* ALFREDO.]

ALFREDO: It's only me. Good morning, gentlemen.

MAX [*pointing to* ALFREDO'S *station*]: The veal is there.

ALFREDO [*studying the menu on the board*]: Thank you, thank you.

PAUL [*shouting*]: Is the new cook here?

ALFREDO [*shrugging his shoulders*]: He didn't ask for me.

[*Enter* MONIQUE *with glasses.*]

PAUL: I thought you said Marango's coming.

MONIQUE: I said he's in the dining-room – he's still there.

RAYMOND: Monique, what happened last night, you tell us?

MONIQUE: No more Ray, there's a good man. Gaston has a black eye.

PAUL: A right morning we're going to have this morning then.

RAYMOND: And Peter – nothing?

MONIQUE: He was lucky.

RAYMOND: You mean he was with you so they couldn't touch him.

MONIQUE: I mean he was lucky. They waited for him outside.

RAYMOND: Outside also?

MONIQUE: 'You want to play gangsters?' he says to them, 'Go bring me Marlon Brando and I'll play gangsters.'

RAYMOND: A time like that he's funny.

MONIQUE: And then he shakes hands with them and says 'Goodnight, bonne nuit, gute Nacht and Kalinka' one by one. And he leaves them all standing. [*Smiles.*] What could they do? [*Smile fades.*] The bully!

HEAD WAITER: Monique ... [*As he enters from dining-room.*]

MONIQUE: Morning, Harry.

HEAD WAITER: Janey is sick.

MONIQUE: Not again. That girl's anaemic, I swear she's anaemic.

HEAD WAITER: Take over for the day, please.

MONIQUE: But I'm not dressed for hostess.

HEAD WAITER: That dress looks all right to me – just take off the apron.

MONIQUE: This one? But it's not ironed!

HEAD WAITER: You only have to show the customers to their tables, not dance with them. [*Exits.*]

MONIQUE: That's three times this week I've been hostess. Here Bertha, look after this apron for me.

BERTHA: Give it me Tchooch, I'll sit on it and keep it pressed.

[*Enter* DAPHNE, GWEN *and* HETTIE.]

MONIQUE: Hettie, Janey's sick again, take over my station will you love? Daphne, give her a hand will you?

DAPHNE: I'm on glasses don't forget.

MONIQUE: True ... I forgot. Who's left then? Winnie's on ten. Gwen's on ... Gwen, what station you on today?

GWEN: Seven.

MONIQUE: Seven ... That's your hands full.

HETTIE: What about the new woman?

MONIQUE: Good idea, she's an old hand isn't she? She can help you, and you can keep an eye on her – come on, let's move.

PAUL: And the best of British luck.

MONIQUE: At least it means I won't have to stand in front of that bully all day.

[*The waitresses all exit.*]

PAUL: Fancy that sort of relationship?

RAYMOND: Peter and Monique? They're not so bad – it's her husband I wouldn't like to be.

PAUL: No, you wouldn't.

RAYMOND: There – I've done it again. I'm sorry Paul.

PAUL: That's all right, I don't mind being cuckolded, I'm in good company.

[*Enter* MICHAEL.]

MICHAEL [*to* BERTHA]: Morning, fatty. How are you?

BERTHA: And you can shut up for a start, little boy. I can ring your napkins out any day. With you tucked in them, any day.

[*Enter* GASTON.]

MICHAEL [*to* GASTON]: Your eye's black.

GASTON: YOU TELLING ME SOMETHING.

MICHAEL: All right, all right . . . whew . . . He looked as though he wanted to kill me.

PAUL: Who'd want to kill you, Michael?

MICHAEL: Quite right . . . who'd want to kill me? Young man in his teens, all the world in front of him. Look at it . . . a lovely sight, isn't it? Isn't she beautiful? A bloody great mass of iron and we work it – praise be to God for man's endeavour – what's on the menu today? I don't know why I bother – it's always the same. Vegetable soup, minestrone, omolletteeee au jambon – ah well! One day I'll work in a place where I can create masterpieces, master bloody pieces. Beef Stroganoff, Chicken Kiev, and that king of the Greek dishes – Moussaka.

GASTON: Never. You'll never create a Moussaka. Chips you can make – chips with everything.

MICHAEL: Don't you think you Greeks have got the monopoly on good cooking, you know. There was a time when the English knew how to eat.

GASTON: There was a time.

MICHAEL: Aye – well – yes – there was a time.

[*Enter* HANS, *who escorts* KEVIN. *Sooner or later they all arrive to glance at the menu on the blackboard.* NICHOLAS *follows them to his station.*]

HANS [*to* KEVIN]: I not know where you work. On fish perhaps. [*To* Paul] Paul, new cook.

PAUL: Hello.

[*They continue to work while* KEVIN *watches them and the rest of the kitchen.*]

KEVIN: Is there much doing here?

PAUL: You'll see. Two thousand customers a day.

[*While* KEVIN *has been introduced and is talking to the pastrycooks,* BERTHA *goes to the cold cupboard and, after looking around inside, takes out a tray of sliced, cold potatoes. Following behind, about to start his work, is* NICHOLAS. *He has a bottle of beer in his hand, which he is drinking.*]

NICHOLAS [*to* BERTHA]: Where you go with that?

BERTHA: I need it for sauté.

NICHOLAS [*taking tray*]: Oh, no, no, no. That's for me. Me, I prepared that yesterday. That's for me for my salad.

BERTHA [*trying to hold on to tray*]: You get your salad from the veg room.

NICHOLAS: Ah no bloody hell! You get *yours* from the veg. That is for me, that is what I get ready.

BERTHA [*nastily*]: You don't bloody hell me, my son. You bloody hell in your own country. [*To others*] What d'you think of him, eh? The little . . .

NICHOLAS: This is my country.

BERTHA: The lavatory is your country.

NICHOLAS [*taking tray eventually*]: The lavatory is *your* country, and the sewers, you know that? The sewers.

BERTHA [*taking out another tray*]: I'll pay you sonny. You cross me once, that's all, just once. Lousy little foreigner you!

NICHOLAS [*cheekily*]: *She* calls *me* foreigner! Listen to her . . .

ALFREDO [*approaching cupboard for his own goods*]: Excuse me friends, you can carry on in a minute. [*But the quarrel has died down.*]

NICHOLAS [*approaching pastry-section*]: D'you hear her? Uh? The cow! Paul, you got some tart or cake or something? I'm starving. [PAUL *hands him tart.*] [*To* KEVIN] You the new cook?

KEVIN: Yes.

NICHOLAS: Good luck to you! [*Laughs to the others*] You know where your station is?

KEVIN: I don't even know what stations there are.

NICHOLAS: Here, I'll show you. Right now for a start there's the menu ... That's where you find what to cook for day, our chef writes it out each night. Over here, this is where I work on the Cold Buffet. This is Max the Butcher. This is where Hans works, he does Staff and Rice and Cutlets and you know, and this is Alfredo on the Roast. And next here, we got the Second Chef Frank on Poultry ... And here, well here you see that fat bitch down there, well she works here as the Veg Cook. And this is my Aunty Anne who is on the Teas and Coffees. This is Michael on Soups and Omelets. And this is my best friend Gaston, the best cook in this kitchen, he does Steaks and Chops. Co-Co works here but he's off today. Here are Paul and Raymondo, Pastrycooks. And here, this is where Peter works on Boiled Fish, he ...

> [*By this time he has to take* KEVIN *back to left of stage and point out the other stations. As he talks on,* PETER *enters in a great hurry, he is late. He laughs his laugh.*]

PETER: Auf geht's! Auf geht's!

HANS: Auf geht's, Pete! Was war denn los heut' Morgen?

PETER: Ach die Weiber! Die Weiber!

NICHOLAS: Peter, the new cook, I give him to you.

PETER: So what shall I do with him? [*To* KEVIN] You know where it is you work?

KEVIN: Not yet I don't.

PETER: Where do you come from?

KEVIN: Ireland.

PETER: No, I mean what restaurant you work in before?

KEVIN: Parisito, Shaftesbury Avenue.

PETER [*rubbing his thumb and finger together*]: Good pay?

KEVIN [*shaking his head*]: That's why I came here.

PETER: Oh, you get good money here — but you work! [*raising his hands in despair*] Oh yes! Now, you help me. Can you make a sauce hollandaise? You know — eggs and ... [*Makes motion of whisking.*]

KEVIN: Yes, yes.

PETER [*briskly*]: The eggs are already in a tin in the cold cupboard. There is a pot, the whisk is in the drawer and I melt margarine for you.

> [*By now almost everybody is working. Waitresses are making an appearance, they are carrying glasses back and forth; one,* CYNTHIA,

is handing out the printed menu for the day, another is taking round bread for lunch for the kitchen staff. As she reaches HANS, *he approaches her shyly and tries to flirt with her.*]

HANS: Oh baby, wait a moment! I ... I ... I ... Du gefällst mir, du hast mir schon vom ersten Tag angefallen! Könnten wir nicht mal was zusammen arrangieren?

[FRANK, *the second chef, enters and breaks up conversation.*]

MAX [*to* FRANK]: We got no lamb cutlets.

FRANK: Three carcasses came in yesterday.

MAX: So?

FRANK: So!

MAX: So you come and help me cut them up. I'm on my own today.

FRANK: What you got?

MAX: Veal cutlets.

FRANK: O.K., so veal cutlets then. [*Moving to* KEVIN] New cook?

KEVIN [*sweating and still beating his sauce*]: Yes, Chef.

FRANK: Right, you work on the fried fish this morning.

PETER [*approaching from cutting-table*]: Thank you, thank you, but I got six dishes to prepare.

FRANK: Co-Co is off today. Someone must do the fry.

PETER: Bloody house this is. The middle of summer and we got no staff. I got six dishes.

[The CHEF *enters.*]

ALFREDO: Morning, Chefie.

CHEF: Morning.

MAX: Morning, Chef.

CHEF: Morning.

HANS [*cheekily*]: Morning, Chefie.

[*The* CHEF *stops, turns, looks* HANS *up and down, then continues to his desk.* HANS *pulls a face, and makes a rude sign.*]

FRANK: Morning, Leo. [*To* KEVIN] Here, you, get that fish out of that cupboard and come here, I want to show you something.

HANS [*to* PETER]: Du, gestern Abend hat's dich aber beinah erwischt!

PETER: Sie sind nur mutig, wenn sie zusammen sind!

HANS: Haben sie draussen auf dich gewartet?

PETER: Ja, da waren auch welche. Leider war ich mit Monika zusammen und jetzt spricht sie nicht mehr mit mir.

HANS: Sie wird auch wieder mit dir reden!

PETER: Ach egal! Auf geht's! [*Sings his song, in which* HANS *joins him, ending in laughter.*] Hi lee, hi lo, hi la!

GASTON [*passing at that moment*]: Madmen, lunatics!

PETER: Hey Gaston, I'm sorry – your black eye, I'm sorry about it.

GASTON: DON'T TALK TO ME.

PETER: I say I'm sorry, that's all.

GASTON: You sorry because half a dozen Cypriot boys make you feel sorry – but we not finished yet!

PAUL: Gaston! What's the matter with you? A man is saying sorry – so accept!

GASTON: Accept? He gives me this [*pointing to black eye*] and I must accept? [*To* PETER] We not finished yet, I'm telling you.

PETER: What you not finished with? Tell me! What you want to do now? You want to give me a black eye? That make you feel happier? All right! Here, give me one and then we'll be finished, eh? [*Adopts quixotic stance.*]

GASTON: Don't laugh, Peter, I'm telling you, it gets worse, don't laugh.

[PETER *adopts another quixotic stance.*]

PAUL [*to* PETER]: So what are you tantalizing him for? Lunatic! [*To* RAYMOND] Nobody knows when to stop. A quarrel starts and it goes on for months. When *one* of them is prepared to apologize so the other doesn't know how to accept – and when someone knows how to accept so the other . . . ach! Lunatics! [*Throws a hand of disgust, while* PETER *sings loudly.*]

[MONIQUE *approaches* GASTON *and lays a friendly arm on his shoulder as they both watch* PETER'S *antics.*]

MONIQUE: He makes a lot of noise but he's not really dangerous.

GASTON: Listen to him – your boy-friend!

MONIQUE: Show me the eye. Beautiful! First prize!

GASTON: Now Monique, don't protect him.

MONIQUE: But you know he wouldn't hurt anyone – not intentionally.

GASTON: This eye –

MONIQUE: It was an accident, you know it was, just between us you know it was, don't you? Why don't you just let me try and handle him?

GASTON: You? You're like a bit of paper – the wind blows you about.

MONIQUE: I manage.

GASTON: Manage? What sort of a life is manage? Manage! He needs a big scare, a big fright.

MONIQUE: Fright? Nothing frightens that boy.

GASTON: Boy! A baby! You just threaten to leave him and you'll see how frightened he'll get.

MONIQUE: I've threatened. But it doesn't scare, only angers him. Angers him, confuses me, frustrates us both. That's our relationship. And I'm no help, really. A weak, indecisive thing, me. Made for comfort, not crisis.

GASTON: Listen to him – baby!

[*The* HEAD WAITER *enters to* CHEF'*s desk.*]

HEAD WAITER [*handing* CHEF *a letter*]: Read it.

CHEF: What's this one about?

HEAD WAITER: Read it. Read it.

CHEF: Sour soup, what sour soup?

HEAD WAITER: Yesterday's.

CHEF: I was off yesterday, see Frank.

HEAD WAITER [*mumbling to himself*]: He was off yesterday ... A kitchen he runs. [*Goes to* FRANK.]

FRANK: What do you want? Nicholas! Twelve chickens.

NICHOLAS: There are only six.

FRANK: Well order some more! What's this sour soup ...?

HANS: Auf geht's, Nicholas! Come on, Nicholas! Twelve chickens, please! Bonjour Raymond, comment ça va?

RAYMOND: Ça va, toujours au boulot, etcetera.

HANS: Vive le frigue!

MAX [*suddenly and violently to* HANS]: You're in England now, speak bloody English. [HANS *is nonplussed for the day.*] Everybody speaking in a different language, French, Italian, German. [*To* HANS] You come here to learn English didn't you? Well speak it then!

PETER: What's the matter Max? You frightened of something? Have another beer.

MAX: I'm not frightened of you, I tell you that straight. So *you* can keep quiet.

PETER [*approaching close to* MAX *and talking in his ear*]: You know your trouble Max? You been here too long.

MAX [*moving away from him*]: Yes, yes, yes Peter, all right.

PETER [*following him*]: How long have you been here? Twenty-one years? You need a change.

MAX: [*moving away again*]: Yes, yes.

PETER [*following him*]: Why don't you go work a season in Germany?

MAX: Sure to.

PETER: Visit other kitchens! Learn more!

MAX: Yes, yes. Get on with your work.

PETER: Don't you worry about my work!

HANS: Genug, Pete.

PETER: You can't bear a change? A new face upsets you?

MAX: Let's drop it? Erwigt yes?

HANS: Stop it, Pete!

CHEF: All right, Peter – let's have some work!

[MR MARANGO *appears*.]

HANS: Marango!!

[PETER *returns to his work and winks at* RAYMOND *in passing.* MARANGO *walking slowly round the kitchen inspecting everything, placing his hand on the hot-plate to see if it is still working. It is a mechanical movement – sometimes he puts a hand on the cold pastry slab to see if it is still hot – it is a mechanical tour. Meanwhile –*]

KEVIN [*to* PETER]: Is it like this every day? [*Wiping sweat from forehead.*] Look at me, I never sweated so much since me glorious honeymoon.

PETER: It is nothing this. This is only how it begins. Wait till we start serving, then. [*Raises his hands.*] You in place?

KEVIN: More or less. I got me salmon to cut.

PETER: Good, we eat soon.

MARANGO [*gently to* KEVIN]: You're the new cook?

KEVIN [*wiping his brow again*]: Yes sir.

MARANGO: It's hot eh, son?

KEVIN: Sure, an' a bit more.

MARANGO: Never mind, I pay you well. Just work, that's all, just work well. [*Continues tour.*]

KEVIN [*to* PETER]: He seems a kind old man.

PETER: You think he is kind? He is a bastard! He talks like that because it is summer now. Not enough staff to serve all his customers, that is why he is kind. You going to stay till winter? Wait till then. You'll see. The fish is burnt! Too much mise-en-place! The soup is sour! He is a man? He is a restaurant! I tell you.

He goes to market at five thirty in the morning; returns here, reads the mail, goes up to the office and then comes down here to watch the service. Here he stands, sometimes he walks round touching the hot-plate, closing the hot-plate doors, then looking inside this thing and that thing. Till the last customer he stays. Then he has a sleep upstairs in his office. Half an hour after we come back, he is here again – till nine thirty, maybe ten at night. Every day, morning to night. What kind of a life is that, in a kitchen! Is that a life I ask you? Me, I don't care, soon I'm going to get married and then whisht – [*Makes movement with his arm to signify 'I'm off.'*]

HANS [*approaches with large tray in his hand which he later puts in cold cupboard*]: Auf geht's, Irishman! I must not speak German to you. I'm in England and have to speak *bloody* English. Hi lee, hi lo, hi la!

[*At this point,* MONIQUE *passes by where* PETER *is working. She is carrying glasses.*]

MONIQUE [*to* PETER]: Bully!

PETER [*to* MONIQUE]: Go to hell! [*To* KEVIN *proudly*] That's my wife, or she will be soon. Look [*takes out card from wallet*] – this card she sent me when she was on holiday. [*Reading aloud.*] 'I am not happy till you come. I love you very much.' And look, her lipstick marks. She is very lovely, yes?

KEVIN: She looks like a girl I knew, all bosom and bouncing you know?

PETER [*not really understanding what* KEVIN *said*]: We eat soon, eh? [KEVIN *goes of to pursue his printed menu.*] [*To* HANS] Hans, hilf mir. [*They take a large heavy pot off from the oven, and pass the contents through a strainer into a small pot which* PETER *has prepared on the ground.*]

KEVIN [*showing menu to* PETER]: Look here, it says on the printed menu fried plaice and on the board it says fried sole.

PETER: See the Chef.

KEVIN [*approaching* CHEF]: Good morning, Chef. Look, it says here fried plaice and on the board it's got fried sole.

CHEF: I don't know anything about it. It was my day off yesterday, see the Second Chef.

KEVIN: Have we got any plaice?

CHEF [*sarcastically looking inside his apron*]: It's not here.

KEVIN [*moves away to* RAYMOND]: Now that's a helpful person for you. Doesn't he care about anything:

RAYMOND: He don't want to know nothing, only when it's gone wrong.

[MONIQUE *again passes in front of* PETER *to glassery.* PETER *is angry. Tries to make his quarrel secret but of course this is impossible.*]

PETER: Why do you still call me bully, all day you call me bully.

MONIQUE [*moves away across front of stage*]: Bully!

PETER [*following her and talking, as is his habit, in her ear*]: You think to make me angry? What is it you wanted me to do? Let him fight me?

MONIQUE [*turning to him at last*]: He's got a black eye now you see?

PETER: I see, I see. But he raised a knife to me.

MONIQUE: Bully. [*She turns away.*]

PETER [*following her like the pathetic, jealous lover*]: And remember you're hostess today, I can see you in the glass. No flirting, do you hear? [*Grips her arm.*] No flirting.

MONIQUE: I shall talk to who I like. [*Moves off.*]

PETER [*hoping no one can hear him*]: Cow! Disgusting cow! All the restaurant can see you.

[*At this point,* HANS *draws out the table from the pastry-section more to the centre of the stage, and begins to lay it with cutlery and glasses and bread, ready for lunch.* MAX, ALFREDO, NICHOLAS *and* FRANK *prepare to eat at* MAX'S *table.* KEVIN, MICHAEL, PETER *and* HANS *will eat at the table* HANS *is now laying.* GASTON *will not eat because he will not sit with* PETER. *These two continue to ignore each other throughout the day.*]

MICHAEL [*shouting*]: Who has the strainer? Gaston? Peter?

PETER: I got it here, you'll have to clean it. [*To a kitchen porter who is near by*] Hey, Mangolis, you clean this for Michael please?

[MANGOLIS *makes a rude sign with his hand and moves off.* PETER *shrugs his shoulder, and* MICHAEL *heaves up strainer himself, and carts it off.* HETTIE *stops in her work to speak to* PETER.]

HETTIE [*as though to confide in him only*]: Hey, Peter, what happened last night, they didn't . . .?

PETER [*briskly, as she only wants to gossip*]: No, no. Cowards, all of them. It was nothing.

PAUL [*to same waitress as she passes his section*]: Hettie, did you go last night?

HETTIE [*ecstatically*]: Mmm.

PAUL: He's a good actor?

HETTIE [*even more. ecstatically and hugging herself*]: What a man. Oh one night, just one night with him, and then I wash dishes all my life. [*Moves off.*]

RAYMOND [*to* PAUL]: So what chance do we stand? You wonder my wife doesn't make love like she used to?

PAUL: And that's why I'm not going to get married. I buy picture books and I'm happy.

GWEN: All right boys, staff meal, coming up.

[*While* PAUL *and* RAYMOND *are talking, a long procession of straggling, gossiping and giggling waitresses have come down stage on the left and are moving around to* HANS *and* ALFREDO, *who have laid trays of food on the serving-counters. Beside food are piles of plates. The waitresses help themselves.*]

GWEN: What've you got for us this morning?

ALFREDO: Curried cats and dogs.

GWEN: Is this cabbage from yesterday?

HANS: It's all right, it's all right, eat it, eat.

VIOLET: What are these?

HANS: Very good, very good. Cauliflower and white sauce.

VIOLET: White sauce? It smells.

MOLLY: Got anything good, Hans?

HANS: If you don't like – go to Chef.

MOLLY: Got any boiled potatoes?

HANS: Not cooked yet, not ready, ach . . .

[HANS *moves away in disgust leaving them to serve themselves. He watches* PETER *working a second, and then goes into steam-room. As the waitresses are serving themselves and grumbling and eventually moving off to the dining-room, we discover that* NICHOLAS *has been arguing with* DAPHNE. *He is making his quarrel much too public for her liking. He is probably a little drunk already.*]

NICHOLAS: Me? Me? Me a liar?

DAPHNE: Yes, you.

NICHOLAS: Oh! So I lied when I say I pass the catering exams, eh? I lie when I say I got a rise, eh? I lie when I say I got us a flat, eh? I always *do* and you always say I don't. That's a good marriage is it?

DAPHNE: You're not satisfied? Move!

NICHOLAS: Well listen to that twist! Listen-to-that-woman's-twisting! Come and ask him then, come on. You don't believe *me*, believe *him* then.

DAPHNE: No, Nicky, no . . . now stop.

NICHOLAS: Well, why don't you believe me then? If I tell you I got to stay the afternoon, why don't you believe me? [*Shouting.*] Frank! Frank! Where is he now. [*Wanders off in search of Frank while waitress waits wondering what he is going to do.*]

RAYMOND [*shouting to waitress*]: Hit him! Go on, you're big enough. [*Nudges* PAUL, *they laugh.*]

FRANK [*as he is dragged into the scene by* NICHOLAS]: What do you want me for? What is it now, eh?

DAPHNE: Oh Nicky, don't be a fool. [*To* RAYMOND *and* PAUL *despairingly.*] Oh for Christ's sake, what do you think of him now!

NICHOLAS: No, ask him, go on. You don't believe me.

FRANK: Ask him what, for hell's sake?

NICHOLAS: Have I got to work in the afternoon or haven't I?

FRANK [*moving away, incredulous that he has been called away for this*]: You called me for *that*? You mad or something? Do me a favour and leave me out of this, will you. [*Grinning to the others.*] Asks me to solve his marriage problems. [*To* NICHOLAS] I'll tell you how to do it as well, ha, ha, ha!

[*Crashing in on laughter is a loud scream from the steam-room.* HANS *comes running out with his hands covering his face. A number of people run and crowd him.*]

HANS: My face! My face! I burnt my face.

FRANK: What is it Hans?

HANS: Who bloody fool put a pot of hot water on steamer?

PETER: It fell on you?

HANS [*moving away from crowd*]: Bastard house! I never worked before so bad. Never, never . . . [PETER *takes him away for some first aid.*]

FRANK: He'll live. [*To the crowd*] All right, it's all over, come on. [*Crowd disperses.* FRANK *moves over to* CHEF.]

MOLLY [*calling after them*]: Put some of that yellow stuff on him.

FRANK: No matter how many times you tell them they still rush around.

CHEF [*he is not interested, shrugs shoulders*]: Is the new chap all right?

FRANK: He seems to be. Look out. [MARANGO *approaches.*]

MARANGO: How did it happen?

CHEF [*as though concerned*]: I don't know. I wasn't there. Frank, how did it happen?

FRANK [*wearily*]: Someone left a pot of boiling water on one of the steamers and he tipped it over his face.

MARANGO: He's burnt his face. It's not serious, [*to* CHEF] but it might have been. [*He shakes his head sadly and moves away.*]

CHEF: What can I do, Mr Marango? They rush about like mad, I tell them but they don't listen.

[MARANGO *moves off shaking his head still.*]

CHEF [*to* FRANK]: Much he cares. It interrupts the kitchen so he worries. Three more years, Frank, three, that's all and then whisht! Retire, finish! Then you can take over.

FRANK: Oh no! Not this boy. I'm in charge one day a week – enough! They can find another madman.

CHEF: Do you think I'm mad?

FRANK: Do you enjoy your work?

CHEF: Who does?

FRANK: So on top of not enjoying your work you take on responsibility – that isn't mad?

CHEF: I've got a standard of living to keep up – idiot!

FRANK [*moving off*]: So go mad!

CHEF: Idiot! Michael!

MICHAEL: Chef?

CHEF: The soup was sour yesterday.

MICHAEL: Sour?

CHEF: Sour!

MICHAEL: But it was only a day old.

CHEF: I've had letters from customers.

MICHAEL: Customers!

CHEF: And Michael – don't take chickens home with you.

MICHAEL [*innocently*]: Chickens?

CHEF: Take cutlets, take cold meats but not chickens. Chickens are bulky. Wait till you're my age before trying chickens.

MICHAEL: Oh, I must graduate to it like.

CHEF: That's right, you must graduate to it like. You can have your lunch now.

[PETER *and* HANS *return.*]

KEVIN: You all right?

[HANS *makes a movement of his hands to say 'Ach, I'm fed-up, forget it.'*]

PAUL: You look beautiful.

KEVIN: A Red Indian.

PETER: Come on, let's eat.

[*They all move to their places to eat;* PAUL *returns to his work; there is less activity in the kitchen now – the calm before the storm. A few waitresses wander around, a porter sweeps the floor.*]

KEVIN [*to* PETER]: How long have you been here?

PETER: Three years.

[MICHAEL *laughs.*]

KEVIN: How did you stick it?

MICHAEL: Sick all ready?

KEVIN: I don't think I'll last the day.

PETER: People are always coming and going.

HANS [*he is not eating much*]: I think me I'll go soon.

MICHAEL [*to* KEVIN]: The worse is to come. [*To others*] Am I right? You wait till the service, ah! ... But you'll get used to it after a while.

PETER: We all said we wouldn't last the day, but tell me what is there a man can't get used to? Nothing! You just forget where you are and you say it's a job.

MICHAEL: He should work on the eggs. Five dishes I've got, five! Hey Paul, any cakes?

PAUL: They're all gone – I got some tart from yesterday. [*Raising his shoulders*] Sorry!

MICHAEL [*not too loudly*]: Liar!

KEVIN: I thought you could eat what you liked here.

MICHAEL: You can, but you have to swipe it. Even the food for cooking. If I want to make an onion soup that's any good, I go to the cold-room and I take some chickens' wings to make my stock. No questions, just in and out – whisht!

PAUL [*to* RAYMOND]: Why do we say there isn't any cake when there is?

RAYMOND: Don't you worry – they eat plenty.

PAUL: So do we. Have you ever caught yourself saying something you don't mean to say? Why did I refuse Michael a cake? Doesn't hurt me to give him a cake, most times we do but there's always that one time when we don't. First thing in the morning I joke with him and half way through the day I lie to him, defending the governor's property as though it was me own. I don't know what to be bloody loyal to half the time.

PETER: Hey, where's Gaston? Why is he not with us, eating here? I black his eye not his arse.

PAUL: Leave off, Peter – the row's over now, patch it up.

MICHAEL: When husbands and wives can't patch up their rows, who are we to succeed?

PAUL: My wife was a mean-minded woman, Michael. She came from a well-run and comfortable-off home but she was mean-minded. I did right by her so don't you be concerned about that. [FRANK, ALFREDO and MAX *laugh amongst themselves.*] Every time someone asked us how we were she used to say 'Busybody.' Oh yes you can laugh, cocker, but I used to have to spend hours listening to her being bitchy about other women. I tried everything. Hours I spent – I even tried to – aaah what the hell do I bother to explain to you for, here – take your bloody bit of cake.

[*Embarrassed silence.*]

HANS: I think I go to America.

KEVIN: America?

HANS [*grins sheepishly, he is about to surprise* KEVIN]: I been to New York already.

KEVIN: You have?

HANS: I already been twice. [*Nods head to say 'What do you think of that!'*] Worked on a ship. [*Pause.*] On a ship you waste more than you eat. [*Lets this sink in.*] You throw everything into the sea before you come on land. [*Sinks in further.*] Whole chickens! The gulls, you know, they eat it.

KEVIN: What about New York?

HANS [*kissing his fingers*]: New York? New York, das ist die schönste Stadt der Welt! Wenn du ankommst – When you arrive: The skyline! The Empire State Buildings! Coney Island! And Broadway, Broadway – you heard of Broadway? [KEVIN *nods with his mouth full.*] Ah . . . beautiful city.

KEVIN: I heard it, yes.

HANS [*in his stride now. Grimace, meaning – 'No question of it!'*]: And Kevin! Women! Three in the morning! And bars and night-clubs! Rush here and rush there! [*More grimace. Secretly, the others jeer*

35

good-naturedly.] A beautiful city! I think this house not very good
. . . here.

KEVIN: It's not, eh?

PETER [*moving to get glass of water*]: You got to turn out food hot
and quickly. Quality – pooh! No time!

KEVIN: Even in the small restaurants they're not after caring much.

MICHAEL [*lighting cigarette*]: Why should they! It's this [*rubs thumb
and finger together*] that counts, you know that.

KEVIN: Oh I don't know. You'd've thought it was possible to run a
small restaurant that could take pride in its food and made money
too.

PETER: Of course it's possible, my friend – but you pay to eat in it.
It's money. It's all money. The world chase money so you chase
money too. [*Snapping his fingers in a lunatic way*.] Money! Money!
Money!

[PETER *is now near* FRANK. *On an impulse he places glass in the
cup of* FRANK's *tall white hat, and creeps back laughing his laugh
to himself*.]

PETER: Frank!

[FRANK *of course moves and the water spills over him. More laughter from* PETER.]

FRANK [*shouting across to* PETER]: One day you'll lay an egg too
many and it'll crack under you. Yes – you laugh.

PETER: Frank is also unhappy. [GWEN *approaches table*.] Yes?

GWEN [*lays hand on* MICHAEL's *shoulder; he lays his on her buttocks*]:
Who's on fish today?

MICHAEL: Do you love me?

GWEN: I think you're irresistible. Who's on fish?

KEVIN: Me.

GWEN: Right, I order four plaice. [*Moves off*.]

PETER [*easing* KEVIN *back to seat because he has just risen to serve that
order*]: You got time. You not finished your lunch yet. The
customer can wait. [*To* KEVIN.] Be like Mr Alfredo. Nothing dis-
turbs Mr Alfredo. Mr Alfredo is a worker and he hates his boss.
He knows his job but he does no more no less and at the right
time. Mr Alfredo is an Englishman – look at that!

[*At this point* MR ALFREDO *comes to the front of the stage and
looks around to see that no one is watching. No one is. He tucks
something first into the right of his apron. Then, straightening himself*

36

out, he returns to pick his teeth. MOLLY *approaches* FRANK.]

MOLLY: Mr Marango wants a leg of chicken and some sauté.

FRANK: Mr Marango can go to hell, I'm eating.

MOLLY [*moves off*]: I'll call for it in five minutes.

FRANK: They don't give you a chance to eat here.

MAX: Hey, you heard they nearly killed Peter last night?

FRANK: Don't talk to me about that boy. He's mad. I've had too much of him already ... three years.

NICHOLAS: They should kill 'em off! Kill 'em off! The lot! Boche! I hate them, you know? I don't hate no one like I hate them. And they want to abolish hanging now. You read about it?

MAX [*to* FRANK]: Do you think that Bill'll go through?

FRANK: How should I know! I suppose it's worth a try.

MAX: They'll be sorry, I'm telling you.

NICHOLAS [*self-righteously*]: What I say is if a man he kills another then he should be killed too.

MAX [*approvingly*]: An eye for an eye.

NICHOLAS: And we should use the electric chair. It's no good the hanging.

MAX [*enjoying what he is about to say*]: Remember those two they put on the chair in America not long ago, for spying? The bloody thing misfired – ha – they had to do it again. I bet the duty electrician on that job got a rollicking.

FRANK: What do you want them to use – gas ovens?

[MONIQUE *walks past* PETER *to front of stage and waits for him by his station. She has a cup of tea in her hand.* PETER *jumps up and goes to her. They do this every meal-break.*]

PETER: You forgive me?

MONIQUE: I can't keep up a row, I laugh after a while.

PETER: I'm a good boy, really. When's your day off?

MONIQUE: Tomorrow.

PETER: Then I won't see you.

MONIQUE: No.

PETER: What are you going to do?

MONIQUE: In the morning I'm going shopping. In the afternoon I'm going to have my hair done, and in the evening I'm going dancing at the Astra.

PETER: Why do you have to go there? All the prostitutes go there.

MONIQUE: I'm going with Monty.

PETER: Listen Monique. Tell Monty tonight. Ask for a divorce, eh? We can't go on like thieves, we do damage to ourselves, you know that?

MONIQUE: Peter, not here, please. I can't tell him yet.

PETER: Here — inside here [*knocks at his head with his hand*] we do damage. We insult ourselves. I'm not going to wait much longer, you'll see. You think I like this Tivoli?

MONIQUE: Now stop it. Why do you always choose a public place to talk about it? You go on and on, and I keep telling you to give me time. I've promised I will, and I will, so be patient.

PETER: Patient ... me patient? ... You don't believe me I won't wait, do you?

MONIQUE: Please yourself.

PETER [*despairingly*]: What do you want me to do? Do you want to make me something to laugh at? Three years I'm here now, three ...

MONIQUE: Oh, ye gods!

[MONIQUE *leaves him.* PETER *is about to become furious but controls himself.*]

PETER [*shouting*]: Auf geht's, Irishman. Finish now. Auf geht's.

[KEVIN *takes no notice so* PETER *repeats louder.*]

PETER: Auf geht's, Irishman, auf geht's.

KEVIN: All right all right.

[PETER *sings his song, lifting* HANS *to his feet.* HANS, KEVIN *and* PETER *return to their stations.*]

CHEF: O.K., Frank.

FRANK: All right, let's get some work done.

CHEF: All right, Michael. Mangolis clear.

MANGOLIS: Sir.

[*All return to their stations.* CHEF *approaches* KEVIN.]

CHEF: You all right?

KEVIN: Yes, Chef.

CHEF: In place and everything?

KEVIN: Yes, Chef.

CHEF: Let me see. [*Watches* KEVIN *start to work.*] All right, but quicker, quicker, quicker.

PETER: Quicker, quicker, quicker, Irishman.

HANS: Quicker, quicker.

PETER: Watch him now the Irishman, soon he won't know what's happening ... Hya ... Hya, hya. [*He and* HANS *start to sing their song.*]

KEVIN: Does your mother know you're out?

[*The waitresses begin to enter, shouting their orders at the required station. They take plates from hot-plate, cradle them in their arms and order. They appear in greater numbers as the service swings into motion. Queues form in front of first one cook, then another.*]

MOLLY [*to* HANS]: Two veal cutlets.

HANS: Two veal cutlets.

GWEN [*to* PETER]: Four cod ... do we order cod?

PETER: Yes, back in five minutes.

WINNIE [*to* PETER]: Three turbot.

PETER: Three turbot.

CYNTHIA [*to* HANS]: Four veal cutlets.

HANS: Four veal cutlets! Oh baby wait a moment! I ... I ... I ... Hast du dir's überlegt? Gehen wir zusammen aus? Ich lade dich ein! Wir gehen ins Kino und nachher tanzen. Willst du?

CYNTHIA: No, I – have – to – go – and – get – my – plaice. [*Said as to someone who doesn't understand a word of English.*]

HANS: Oh Gott! My cutlets!

DAPHNE [*to* FRANK]: Three legs of chicken.

FRANK: Three legs of chick.

HETTIE [*to* NICHOLAS]: Two chicken salad.

NICHOLAS: Two chicken salad.

HANS [*who has been watching* CYNTHIA]: Oh my cutlets.

CYNTHIA [*to* KEVIN]: Party of eight plaice to begin with.

KEVIN: Eight plaice. She's a worker.

JACKIE [*to* GASTON]: Five grilled chops.

GASTON: Five grilled chops.

DAPHNE [*to* NICHOLAS]: Three French salad.

HETTIE: I was first.

DAPHNE: Special.

NICHOLAS: Three French salad.

MOLLY [*to* GASTON]: Six steaks.

GASTON: Six steaks.

MOLLY [*to* MICHAEL]: Four minestrone.

MICHAEL: Four minestrone.

GWEN [*to* FRANK]: Two roast chicken and sauté.

FRANK: Two roast chicken and sauté.

CYNTHIA [*to* HANS]: These my veal cutlets?

HANS: These are your cutlets! Four Kalbskotletts only for you baby!

CYNTHIA: Oh really!

HANS [*to* PETER]: Wunderbar! Peter look! Wie die geht! Wie die aussieht, die ist genau meine Kragenweite!

PETER [*singing*]: 'Falling in love again.'

KEVIN: Hey Peter, any more plaice?

PETER: In the cold cupboard.

[*In exiting,* KEVIN *knocks into* DAPHNE.]

DAPHNE: Watch it, Irishman.

PETER [*continuing to tease* HANS]: 'Falling in love again.'

HANS: Oh Pete, stop it! Ich weiss nicht, was ich anstellen soll! I speak quite good English already.

VIOLET: Four cod.

[*They obviously don't hear her.*]

HANS: But with her I forget every word.

VIOLET: I said four cod!

HANS [*to* VIOLET]: Shut up, baby! [*To* PETER] She is smashing!!

[VIOLET *goes off.*]

MONIQUE [*to* CHEF]: Chef, complaint, minestrone.

PETER [*to* MONIQUE]: Now remember, don't forget to remember.

MONIQUE: Remember what?

PETER: What are you doing . . . you don't know what you are doing.

CHEF: Michael, the soup is sour.

MONIQUE [*to* PETER]: Your work . . . your work.

[*While she isn't looking,* MICHAEL *tips the soup straight from one bowl into another, and hands the plate to her.*]

BETTY [*to* ALFREDO]: Two roast beef.

ALFREDO: Hold it, hold it.

BETTY: Oh, is it ready?

ALFREDO: Of course it's ready.

PETER: Mangolis, plates!

MANGOLIS: Plates coming up.

GWEN [*to* PETER]: Is my four cod ready?

DAPHNE [*to* NICHOLAS]: One salad.

WINNIE [*to* FRANK]: Two roast pheasant, darling.

FRANK: Oh charming. I love you. You'll have chicken and like it!

HETTIE [*to* HANS]: Two sausages.

JACKIE [*to* ALFREDO]: One roast pork.

ALFREDO: One roast pork.

DAPHNE [*to* KEVIN]: Two plaice. Oh, where the hell is he?
[*Waits for* KEVIN.]

HETTIE [*to* KEVIN]: Three grilled turbot.

JACKIE [*to* PETER]: Two cod.

PETER: Two cod.

DAPHNE [*to* KEVIN]: Two plaice. Come on, come on Irishman.

KEVIN [*re-entering*]: Oh Jesus, Mother of God, and the Holy Virgin.

GASTON [*who is passing at the same time*]: Exo.

DAPHNE [*to* KEVIN]: Two plaice.

MOLLY [*to* HANS]: My veal cutlets ready?

HANS: What do you think?

HETTIE [*to* KEVIN]: Three grilled turbot.

KEVIN: Three grilled turbot.

MOLLY [*to* NICHOLAS]: One lobster, one ham salad.

NICHOLAS: One lobster, one ham.

CYNTHIA [*to* MICHAEL]: Three omelets au jambon.

MICHAEL: Three jambons.

BETTY [*to* GASTON]: Three entrecote steaks.

GASTON: Three entrecote steaks.

ANNE [*to* PAUL]: My fruit flans ready?

PAUL: I'll bring them up, me old darling.

GWEN [*to* NICHOLAS]: Two ham salads.

NICHOLAS: Two ham salads.

GWEN: I want two coffees, Annie love.

ANNE: All right dear.

WINNIE [*to* HANS]: Two veal cutlets.

HANS: Two veal cutlets ... Oh God. Max, veal cutlets and sausages.

MAX: Yes ... all right. [*Takes tray which* HANS *throws to him.*]

GASTON: Max send up steaks and mutton chops quick. [*Almost
hysterical.*]

MAX [*angrily*]: Wait a bloody minute will you!

GASTON [*in panic*]: I got six steaks ordered already.

MAX: So what am I supposed to do?

GASTON [*to nobody in particular*]: Everybody the same in this bloody
house. I've always got a big queue before I start.
[*Returns mumbling.*]

WINNIE [*to* KEVIN]: One plaice please.

KEVIN: One plaice? Right.

BETTY [*to* FRANK]: One roast chicken.

FRANK: One roast chicken.

HANS: Come on, Max.

HETTIE [*to* KEVIN]: Two grilled salmon, do we order it?

KEVIN: Yes, five minutes. Go on, hop it!

JACKIE [*to* KEVIN]: One grilled trout please.

KEVIN [*rushing around*]: Right away!

MOLLY [*to* KEVIN]: Two plaice please.

KEVIN: All right, all right.

PETER [*shouting while he serves*]: Ha-ha! He-he! Ho-ho! They're here! They come.

HETTIE [*to* NICHOLAS]: One chicken, one ham salad.

CYNTHIA [*to* PETER]: One cod.

PETER: One cod.

WINNIE [*to* MICHAEL]: One hamburger.

MICHAEL: One hamburger.

VIOLET: Are my four cod ready?

GWEN [*to* HANS]: One veal cutlet.

PETER [*to* VIOLET]: When did you order them?

HANS: One veal cutlet.

VIOLET: Five minutes ago. I come past and you were talking to Hans – remember?

PETER: I remember nothing. Come back in five minutes. Next?

VIOLET: You weren't listening, that's what it was.

PETER: You ordered nothing, I say.

MOLLY [*to* MICHAEL]: Two minestrone.

PETER: Now come back five minutes' time . . . next.

VIOLET: Well really.

GWEN [*to* PETER]: One steamed turbot.

PETER: One steamed turbot.

BETTY [*to* HANS]: Three veal cutlets please.

HANS [*mimicking*]: Three veal cutlets please.

HEAD WAITER: Violet.

JACKIE [*to* NICHOLAS]: Two ham, one lobster salad.

DAPHNE [*to* ANNE]: Three fruit flan.

HANS [*to* BETTY, *who has waited*]: What's the matter with you . . . you can't see the cutlets cook.

BETTY: Well, last time I waited.

HANS: Well, last time I waited.

BETTY: Oh get lost ... excuse me Harry. [*To* HEAD WAITER, *who is passing.*]

WINNIE [*to* GASTON]: Three steaks.

HEAD WAITER [*to* CHEF]: Ten minutes ago, Violet ordered four cod. They're not ready yet.

[KEVIN, GASTON *and* MICHAEL *call for plates.*]

CHEF: Peter ... the cod not ready yet?

PETER: She's a liar that one, she ordered nothing.

CHEF: Come on, come on.

PETER: One cod, two cod.

DAPHNE [*to* ANNE]: Two coffees.

PETER: Three cod, four cod.

[*As* VIOLET *turns with the plates,* MANGOLIS, *who is passing, knocks her, and the plates fall to the ground.*]

JACKIE [*to* ANNE]: Three coffees.

VIOLET: Oh God, God, God, I can't, I can't.

GWEN: Don't upset yourself, love.

VIOLET: Look at it all, I can't work like this. I'm not used to this way of working.

BETTY [*to* MICHAEL]: One minestrone.

VIOLET: I've never worked like this before, never never.

[*During this the* CHEF *calls* FRANK, *who calls* MANGOLIS, *to clear the broken china.*]

PETER: Too old, too old my sweetheart. Go home old woman – for the young this work – go home.

HANS [*to* PETER]: Oh stop it, shut up.

[PETER *makes a face after* CHEF, *and when it is safe he begins to sing his song while working. Half way through, he breaks off, and rushes to oven. There is something vast and Shakespearian in the way* PETER *moves – he is always wanting to play the fool.*]

GWEN [*to* HANS]: One veal cutlet.

PETER [*to* KEVIN]: Oh God! She burns! The cod! Hya, hya, hya. She burns, Irishman. No good, no good. [*Rushes the frying-pan with the burnt fish to the dustbin, and covers it with paper.*] Ssh, sssh. Hya, hya, hya.

HANS [*to* PETER, *loudly in the midst of his own work*]: That is not too good work, Peter, not good work mein Lieber. Pig's work. [*Laughs and points to* KEVIN, *who has large queue at his station.*] We have busy time, Irishman, yes?

KEVIN: Bloody comedian.

HETTIE [*to* KEVIN]: My salmon ready?

KEVIN: Your what?

HETTIE: Me grilled salmon.

KEVIN: How many do you want?

HETTIE: Two.

CYNTHIA [*to* MICHAEL]: My three omelets.

MICHAEL: Your three omelets.

DAPHNE [*to* KEVIN]: Two salmon.

JACKIE [*to* KEVIN]: Three sardines.

KEVIN: Peter, for God's sake will you give me a hand?

HETTIE [*to* MICHAEL]: Two veg soups.

PETER [*helping* KEVIN]: Let's go Irishman, let's go. The next.

DAPHNE: Two salmon.

PETER: Right.

BETTY [*to* HANS]: My veal cutlets.

HANS: Your veal cutlets.

PETER: And the next?

JACKIE [*to* PETER]: Three sardines.

BETTY [*to* HANS]: Oh come on, lobster-face.

HANS: What does it mean, lobster-face?

PETER: And the next?

WINNIE [*to* PETER]: Three plaice.

HANS [*to* BETTY]: Ein, zwei, drei.

PETER [*to* WINNIE]: One, two three.

BETTY [*to* PETER]: Two plaice.

> [*While* PETER *has been helping* KEVIN, *the following three orders pile up on his unattended station.*]

MOLLY: One turbot.

GWEN: One steamed halibut.

CYNTHIA: Two cod.

MOLLY: Oh come on, Peter.

> [PETER *rushes to his station, laughing like a merry fool going into battle.*]

PETER: Look at this – hya, hya – good morning ladies – and the next . . .

MOLLY [*to* PETER]: One turbot. [PETER *serves her, and cries out* 'Next, next,' *and so on.*]

GWEN [*to* PETER]: One steamed halibut.

JACKIE [*to* FRANK]: Three legs of chicken.

FRANK: Three chicken.

KEVIN [*to* PETER]: I've run out of lemons!

PETER [*with rude indifference*]: Well cut some more then. The next?

KEVIN: Let me borrow your cutting-board then, please. [*He moves to take it from* PETER'*s bench.*]

PETER [*stops his work, and jumping on* KEVIN, *grabs board: in the kitchen it is every man for himself now*]: Oh no, no, no, no my friend. The plate-room, the plate-room, in the plate-room, you'll find them. This is mine, I have need of it.

KEVIN: But I'll give it back in a few seconds.

PETER [*pointing*]: The plate-room. [*Slams his hand down on the board for emphasis; to a waitress –*] What do you want?

KEVIN [*going to plate-room*]: Well, speak a little human like, will yer please?

PETER: No time, no time. Next.

CYNTHIA [*to* PETER]: Two cod.

JACKIE [*to* NICHOLAS]: One cheese salad.

VIOLET [*to* NICHOLAS]: One ham salad. [*Tearfully.*]

BETTY [*to* GASTON]: My steaks ready yet?

VIOLET [*to* ANNE]: A fruit flan and two coffees.

GASTON [*to* BETTY]: About time.

BETTY: I'm sorry.

DAPHNE [*to* FRANK]: Two roast chicken.

FRANK: Two roast chicken.

WINNIE [*to* ALFREDO]: Two roast veal and spaghetti.

JACKIE [*to* MICHAEL]: One prawn omelet.

MICHAEL: One prawn.

GWEN [*to* ALFREDO]: Two roast beef.

ALFREDO: Two roast beef.

MOLLY [*to* KEVIN]: Two sole.

CYNTHIA [*to* KEVIN]: Three plaice.

DAPHNE [*to* GASTON]: Two lamb chops.

HETTIE [*to* MICHAEL]: Two minestrones.

MONIQUE [*to* PETER]: Four cod.

PETER: What?

MONIQUE: Violet's four cod.

MOLLY [*about* KEVIN]: He's never here, this one.

PETER [*to* MONIQUE]: You wait for me afterwards.

MONIQUE: I'll wait for you.

CYNTHIA [*to* KEVIN]: Come on Irishman, my plaice.

BETTY [*to* MICHAEL]: One minestrone.

PETER [*to* MONIQUE]: We go for a stroll.

MONIQUE: Yes, we go for a stroll.

MOLLY [*to* CYNTHIA]: We'll lose all those tips.

GWEN [*to* HANS]: Four veal cutlets.

HANS: Four veal cutlets.

MOLLY [*to* KEVIN]: Me sole, luvvy, where's me sole?

KEVIN [*re-entering*]: Wait a bloody minute, can't you.

MOLLY [*to* KEVIN]: Two.

GWEN [*to* PETER]: Two halibut.

BETTY [*to* MICHAEL]: Three hamburgers.

CYNTHIA [*to* KEVIN]: Three plaice. There's no time for breathing here, you know.

KEVIN: Jesus is this a bloody madhouse.

MICHAEL: Three hamburgers.

NICHOLAS: Plates.

MANGOLIS: Plates.

KEVIN: Have you all gone barking-raving-bloody-mad.

[*At this point all the waitresses have got into a continuous circle of orders round and round the kitchen, as the volume of the ovens increases and the lights slowly fade to blackout. The calls of orders and for plates and more meat, etc., continue through the blackness until the stage is clear and ready for the interlude. The author would prefer there to be no interval at this point but recognizes the wish of theatre bars to make some money.*]

INTERLUDE

Lights fade up on the sound of a guitar.
It is afternoon break. The sounds of the oven are at half. PAUL *and*
RAYMOND *are working in their corner. These are the only two who stay*
through the afternoon. KEVIN *is flat out on his back on a wooden bench,*
exhausted. DIMITRI *is slowly sweeping up.* PETER *is sitting by a table*
waiting for MONIQUE, HANS *is in a corner with a guitar, singing 'Ah*
sinner-man' in German.

KEVIN: Finished! I'm done! I'm boiled! You can serve me up for
supper!

PAUL [*as if ordering a meal*]: Two portions of boiled Irishman please!
With garnish!

RAYMOND [*also calling*]: Two fried tomatoes on his ears, potatoes
round his head, and stuff his mouth with an extra helping of peas.

KEVIN: I'll produce me own gravy! But did you see it? Did-you-see-
that? Fifteen hundred customers, an' half of them eating fish. *I*
had to start work on a Friday!

RAYMOND: It's every day the same, my friend.

KEVIN [*raising himself up*]: Look at me. I'm soaking. Look at this
jacket. I can wring it out. That's not sweat, no man carries that
much water. [*Flopping back again.*] Kevin, you'll drop dead if you
stay. I'm warning you Kevin, take a tip from a friend, hop it! Get
out! You've got your youth Kevin, keep it! This is no place for a
human being – you'll drop dead, I'm telling yous.

DIMITRI: Hey, Irishman, what you grumbling about this place for?
Is different anywhere else? People come and people go, big excitement, big noise. [*Makes noise and gesticulates.*] What for? In the
end who do you know? You make a friend, you going to be all you
life his friend but when you go from here – pshtt! You forget!
Why you grumble about this one kitchen?

PETER: You're a very intelligent boy, Dimitri.

DIMITRI: And you're a bloody fool. I'm not sure I want to talk with you.

KEVIN: Oh not the Gaston row again. All the morning I hear how
Peter give Gaston a black eye. It's the break, no rows please, it's
peace. Can you hear it? It's lovely, it's silence. It's nothing – ahhh!

47

[*Moves.*] Oooh – I'm drowning, in my own sweat. Christ! What a way to die.

DIMITRI [*to* PETER]: A bloody fool you!

[PETER *picks up a cardboard box, and puts it over* DIMITRI'*s head.* DIMITRI *flings it off angrily and is about to throw it back, but he sees* PETER *with his head in his hands. Instead, he takes out a cigarette box, and begins rolling* PETER *a cigarette. He gives the paper to* PETER *to lick, then continues folding it, and hands it to him.*]

PETER: Hey Irishman, I thought you didn't like this place. Why don't you go home and sleep?

KEVIN: Me home is a room and a bed and a painting of the Holy Virgin. It'll always be there.

PETER: Like this place, this house – this too, it'll always be here. That's a thought for you Irishman. This – this madhouse it's always here. When you go, when I go, when Dimitri go – this kitchen stays. It'll go on when we die, think about that. We work here – eight hours a day, and yet – it's nothing. We take nothing. Here – the kitchen, here – you. You and the kitchen. And the kitchen don't mean nothing to you and you don't mean to the kitchen nothing. But Dimitri is right you know – why do you grumble about this kitchen? What about the offices and the factories? There Irishman – what do you say to that?

KEVIN: You want to come in one morning and find it gone?

PETER: Just one morning. Imagine it, eh? Gone. All this gone.

KEVIN: So you'd be out of work!

PETER: So I'd die?

KEVIN: It doesn't worry you I suppose.

HANS: Du träumst schon wieder.

KEVIN: What's he say?

PETER: He say – I'm dreaming.

[PETER *stands up, and begins idly strolling round the kitchen. Picks up dustbin-lid, a long ladle – shield and sword – lunges at* RAYMOND. RAYMOND *picks up a whisk. A few seconds' duel.* PETER *raises his arms in surrender.*]

PETER: Yah! War! Did you used to play like this, at war, with dustbin-lids and things? I did. Yah! Not very good, eh Irishman? War? Kids playing at war grow up peaceful they say, I think not so simple, eh? Me I never liked war games. I had my own group – boys, we'd build things. Castles, huts, camps.

[*During this,* PETER *has taken two dustbins, puts one on the corner of the stove and one on the opposite corner of his hot-plate He then puts a tall container on top of each and saucepans on top of these. Next he puts* DIMITRI's *broom across the top, and hangs dish-cloths on the handles. He then notices a vase of flowers on the Chef's table, and, selecting the largest, he gives the remainder to* PAUL; *he puts his flower through one of the saucepan handles. With his back to the audience, he faces his creation.*]

PAUL: Beautiful, what is it?

PETER: It's my arch, and I was ... And I was ... [*grabbing a long ladle to use as a saluting sword*] I was ein grosser Deutscher Ritter!

HANS: Hey Peter – weisst du noch?

[*At this point* HANS *starts to play the Horst Wessel song on the guitar.* PETER *does the goose-step through his arch while* PAUL *throws flowers over him and* HANS.]

KEVIN [*sings*]: And the Irish Republican Army made muck of the whole bloody lot. Now isn't that something mad, now.

PETER: You think this is madness?

KEVIN: Well, isn't it? Isn't it kids playing and all that carry-on?

PETER: This one says games and that one says dreams. You think it's a waste of time? You know what a game is? A dream? It's the time when you forget what you are and you make what you could be. When a man dreams – he grows, big, better. You find that silly?

HANS: Du bist zu alt, Peter!

PETER: I'm *not* too old, never, never too old, don't tell me that. Too old! When you're dead you're too old. Hey Irishman, you dream, how do you dream, tell us?

KEVIN: You play your own games, Peter, leave me out of it, I'm past it.

PETER: Why are you ashamed of being a child, Irishman? We all friends here, why you ashamed to dream, I give you the chance.

KEVIN: I'm obliged!

PETER: Hey Paul, Raymondo, Dimitri, stop work a minute. You got time. Here, come here. We are all given a chance to dream. No one is going to laugh, we love each other, we protect each other – someone tell us a dream, just to us, no one else, the ovens are low, the customers gone, Marango is gone, it's all quiet. God has given us a chance now, we never have the opportunity again, so dream – someone – who? Dimitri – you, you dream first.

DIMITRI: In this place? With iron around me? And dustbins? And black walls?

PETER [*coaxing*]: Pretend! There's no dustbins, that's a big beautiful arch there. Pretend! The walls are skies, yes? The iron, it's rock on a coast; the tables, [*thinks*] they're rose bushes; and the ovens are the noise of the winds. Look at the lights – stars, Dimitri.

HANS: Peter, du verschwendest deine Zeit!

PETER: So what! So what if I waste time? It's good to be able to waste time. I got another sixty years to live, I can afford it. Dimitri – dream – a little dream, what you see?

DIMITRI: A little, a little er – what you call it – a small house, sort of –

PAUL: A hut?

DIMITRI: No –

KEVIN: A shed?

DIMITRI: That's right, a shed. With instruments, and tools, and I make lots of radios and television sets maybe, and . . .

PETER: Ach no, silly boy. That's a hobby, that's not what you really want. You want more, more, Dimitri –

[DIMITRI *shrugs*.]

PETER: Poor Dimitri – hey Irishman, you – dream.

KEVIN: If you think because I'm Irish I'm going to start prattling on about goblins and leprechauns you've got another think coming –

PETER: No, no, not fairies, a real dream, about men –

KEVIN: But I don't dream of men –

PETER: What then?

KEVIN: Sleep! Sleep me. Most people sleep and dream; me – I dream of sleep!

PETER: What is it with you all? Hans – you, what are your dreams?

[HANS *sings on, as though not answering the question. Then* –]

HANS: Money! Geld, Peter, Geld! With money I'm a good man! I'm generous! I love all the world! Money, Pete! Money! Money! Money! [*Continues singing.*]

PETER: How can you talk of money, Hans, when you're singing?

HANS: Dreaming, mein Lieber, dreaming, dreaming.

PETER: Raymondo?

RAYMOND: Me? Women!

PETER: Which women? Large, small? Happy? Black? Yellow? What kind?

RAYMOND: There *is* more than one kind?

PETER: Raymond – you make me very sad. Paul – you.

PAUL: Do me a favour.

PETER: Please!

PAUL: No. [*Relents.*] Listen, Peter ... I'll tell you something. I'm going to be honest with you. You don't mind if I'm honest? Right! I'm going to be honest with you. I don't like you. Now wait a minute, let me finish. I don't like you! I think you're a pig! You bully, you're jealous, you go mad with your work, you always quarrel. All right! But now it's quiet, the ovens are low, the work has stopped for a little and now I'm getting to know you. I still think you're a pig – only now, not so much of a pig. So that's what I dream. I dream of a friend. You give me a rest, you give me silence, you take away this mad kitchen so I make friends, so I think – maybe all the people I thought were pigs are not so much pigs.

PETER: You think people are pigs, eh?

PAUL: Listen, I'll tell you a story. Next door to me, next door where I live is a bus driver. Comes from Hoxton, he's my age, married and got two kids. He says good-morning to me, I ask him how he is, I give his children sweets. That's our relationship. Somehow he seems frightened to say too much, you know? God forbid I might ask him for something. So we make no demands on each other. Then one day the busmen go on strike. He's out for five weeks. Every morning I say to him 'Keep going mate, you'll win.' Every morning I give him words of encouragement; I say I understand his cause. I've got to get up earlier to get to work but I don't mind. We're neighbours. We're workers together, he's pleased. Then, one Sunday, there's a peace march. I don't believe they do much good but I go, because in this world a man's got to show he can have his say. The next morning he comes up to me and he says, now listen to this, he says 'Did you go on that peace march yesterday?' So I says Yes, I did go on that peace march yesterday. So then he turns round to me and he says, 'You know what? A bomb should have been dropped on the lot of them! It's a pity,' he says, 'that they had children with them cos a bomb should've been dropped on the lot!' And you know what was upsetting him? The march was holding up the traffic, the buses couldn't move so fast! Now I don't want him to say I'm right, I don't want him to agree with what I did, but what terrifies me is that he didn't stop to think that this man helped me in my cause so maybe, only *maybe*, there's something in his cause. I'll talk about it. No! The buses were held up so drop a bomb he says, on the lot! And you should've seen the hate in his eyes, as if I'd murdered his child. Like an animal he looked. And the horror is this – that there's a wall, a big wall between me and millions of people like him. And I think – where will it end? What do you do about it? And I look around me, at the kitchen, at the factories, at the enormous bloody buildings going up with all those offices and all those people in them, and I think, Christ! I think, Christ, Christ, Christ! I agree with you Peter – maybe one morning we should wake up and find them all gone. But then I think: I should stop making pastries? The factory worker should stop making trains and cars? The miner should leave the coal where it is? [*Pause.*] *You* give *me* an answer. You give me your dream.

KEVIN: Hush pâtissier! Hush! It's quiet now. Gently now.

> [HANS *throws one of the red flowers to* PAUL. *There is a long silence.* HANS, *who had stopped playing, now continues. The ovens hum.* PAUL *sticks the flower in his lapel.*]

PETER: I ask for dreams – you give me nightmares.

PAUL: So I've dreamt! Is it my fault if it's a nightmare?

KEVIN: We're waiting for your dream now, Peter boy.

DIMITRI [*jumping up suddenly*]: This is the United Nations, eh? A big conference. Is Russia here, and America and France and England – and Germany too. Is all here. And they got on a competition. Is finished the wars, is finished the rows. Everybody gone home. We got time on our hands. A prize of one million dollars for the best dream. Raymondo he want a new woman every night. I want a workshop. Paul he wants a friend. Irishman he wants a bed and Hans he just want the million dollars. Big opportunity! Come on Peter, a big dream.

PETER [*looking around*]: All this gone?

DIMITRI: You said so. One morning you come here, to this street here, and the kitchen is gone. And you look around for more kitchens and is none anywhere. What you want to do? The United Nations wants to know.

PAUL: Come on, come on!

PETER: Shush, shush!

[PETER *suddenly confronted with his own idea becomes embarrassed and shy. He laughs.*]

PETER: I can't. I can't.

[MONIQUE *arrives and* PETER *forgets everything and becomes the all-consumed lover, the excited child.*]

MONIQUE: Ready?

PETER: Finished? I come I come. Hey Irishman, you'll soon be coming back. Go home. Change. You catch pneumonia. [*Excitedly*] Auf geht's, auf geht's!

[*The mad* PETER *rushes out with his* MONIQUE. *The rest are left. The guitar and the hum of the ovens.*]

DIMITRI [*shouting at the absent* PETER]: Fool! Bloody fool! We wait for a dream.

PAUL: I don't know what you see in him.

DIMITRI: I don't know what I see in him either. Bloody fool!

KEVIN: Bloody volcano if you ask me. I'm away. [*Rises.*]

PAUL [*returning to his work*]: He hasn't got a dream.

KEVIN: It's all mad talk if you ask me. I don't see no point in it. I don't see no point in that Peter bloke either. He talks about peace and dreams and when I ask him if I could use his cutting-board to cut me lemons on this morning he told me – get your own. Dreams? See yous!

[KEVIN *exits.* HANS *is still playing.* DIMITRI *returns to his sweeping.*]

PAUL [*to* DIMITRI]: So *you* tell me the point of all that. I don't even know what I was saying myself.

DIMITRI: Why should I know? Sometimes things happen and no one sees the point – and then suddenly, something else happen and you see the point. Peter not a fool! You not a fool! People's brain moves all the time. *All* the time. I'm telling you.

[DIMITRI *sweeps on.* HANS *finishes his song, rises, bows, slings his guitar and exits.*

This next scene happens very, very slowly to denote the passing of the afternoon.]

PAUL: Best part of the day.

RAYMOND: When they're gone I slow down.

PAUL: [*throwing a cigarette end to* DIMITRI]: Here's another bit of debris for you. Longest part of the day though, isn't it?

RAYMOND [*offering to* PAUL *from Nicholas's table*]: Tomato? Carrot?

Cucumber? [PAUL *declines all.*] Yes, the longest part.

[*Enter* MANGOLIS. DIMITRI *strikes the bench and table and part of the arch. The afternoon is over.* MANGOLIS *is singing a Greek air;* GASTON *enters followed by* NICHOLAS, *and the four of them gradually start a Greek dance . . .*]

PART TWO

... At the end of the Greek dance, DIMITRI *starts to kick a cardboard box, as in football;* MICHAEL, *entering, intercepts it.*

MICHAEL: And that great little inside left, Michael Dawson, has the ball again. Will he miss this golden opportunity? Can he hold his own against the great Arsenal backs? He *does*! Yes! Past Wills, past MacCullough, past Young and he's going to shoot, he *shoots!* – and it's a goal, a goal, yes, his fifth goal, making the score Leyton Orient eighteen, Arsenal nil. What a game! What a boy! Look at this place, like a battlefield, grrr – it smells of the dead.

[MONIQUE *enters, slamming the door, and exits into the dining-room, in a furious temper.*]

PAUL: Well, they started the afternoon happy. Did you have a good afternoon, Michael?

MICHAEL: Too bloody good ... St James Park. Lying in the sun. Dozing. The girls – aaaah! Hey, I saw Nick and Daphne in the park.

PAUL: There's nice for you.

MICHAEL: Rowing on the lake.

RAYMOND: How touching. Aaaaaah!

MICHAEL: He wasn't doing the rowing though! You boys are lucky, not having to break in the afternoon, come back to work.

PAUL: I thought you liked the place.

MICHAEL: I don't mind the coming in, it's the coming back. Not old Alfred though. Look at him – in, out, cook, serve – he doesn't mind.

[ALFREDO *has entered and gone straight to his work. Following him is* PETER, *who hangs back.*]

ALFREDO: Well come on Peter boy, work, it won't hurt you. Come on then, stock up, replenish, boy.

PETER: My arch – where is it? Who took it down, who took my arch away? Let it stay – let Marango see it.

[GASTON *is emptying waste into one dustbin.*]

PETER [*to* GASTON]: You leave it! You leave it!

[ALFREDO *approaches him. During this conversation the others enter.*]

ALFREDO: You are not ill, are you?

PETER: Who knows.

ALFREDO: No pain nor nothing?

PETER: No. Alfredo, look –

ALFREDO: Good! You have all your teeth?

PETER: Yes.

ALFREDO: Good! You have good lodgings?

PETER: Yes.

ALFREDO: So tell me what you're unhappy for.

PETER: Alfredo, you are a good cook, uh? You come in the morning, you go straight to work, you ask nobody anything, you tell nobody anything. You are ready to start work before we are, you never panic. Tell me, is this a good house?

ALFREDO [*drily*]: Depends. It's not bad for Mr Marango, you know.

MICHAEL [*approaching* PETER]: Peter, give me a cigarette please!

[PETER *does so.* MICHAEL *stays on to listen.*]

ALFREDO: I'm an old man. It's finished for me. Mind you I've worked in places where I could do good cooking. But it doesn't matter now. Now I work only for the money.

MICHAEL: Quite right! A match Peter please.

PETER [*to* MICHAEL, *looking for matches*]: You like it here, don't you?

MICHAEL: The ovens –

PETER: No, I got no matches.

MICHAEL: I love the sound of the ovens. Nick, got a light?

[NICHOLAS *throws him matches.*]

PETER: Idiot! He loves the sound of the ovens! You stand before them all day! They're red hot! You fry first a bit of ham and an egg in a tin; then someone orders an onion soup and you put soup and bread and cheese in another tin, and you grill that; then someone orders an omelet and you rush to do that; then someone throws you a hamburger and you fry that. You go up you go down you jump here you jump there, you sweat till steam comes off your back.

MICHAEL [*moving across to* NICHOLAS *for a light*]: I love it.

PETER [*returning head to arms*]: Good luck to you.

56

ALFREDO [*to* MONIQUE]: Here, you talk to him – he's your genera-tion. [*Moves off.*]

PAUL [*to* RAYMOND]: Come on Lightning, let's get some work done.

MONIQUE [*to* PETER]: Are you still sulking? It was your fault we rowed, not mine, you're just like a little boy.

[*The* CHEF *and* FRANK *enter. The* CHEF *breaks between* PETER *and* MONIQUE.]

PETER: Would you like me old and fat, like your husband? Then you'd have to find a new lover! I sympathize with Monty some-times.

MONIQUE: You feel sorry for him?

PETER: Would you like me to hate him? I can't! I try but I can't, it would be easier but I can't. A good man, kind and no vices – who can hate such persons?

MONIQUE: I'm sorry I left you standing in the street.

PETER: You're always sorry afterwards, like a dog she leaves me.

MONIQUE: Where did you go?

PETER: Never mind – I went. Go on, go. Go wipe your glasses, it's nearly time. Go, leave me.

MONIQUE: Look at you. Look at you ... is it any wonder I don't know where the hell I am ... you behave like this. I come to apologize, I say I'm sorry, I speak reasonably and now you ... you ... [*Exits.*]

[*Enter* DAPHNE *and* HETTIE, *giving out new menus.*]

KEVIN: I'll be taking *my* leave tonight by Christ.

GASTON: You'll get used to it. It's good money.

[*Enter* VIOLET *chatting with* ANNE, *followed by* HEAD WAITER, *who goes to* CHEF'S *table.*]

KEVIN: To hell with the money an' all. I like me pay but not for this. It's too big here, man, it's high pressure all the time. An' the food! Look at the food! I never cooked so bad since I was in the army. An' no one is after caring much either!

VIOLET: And what about the waitresses, we're the animals, everybody pushing everybody else out of the way.

HEAD WAITER: Never mind, Violet. You got over your first morning all right. This evening won't be so bad, nobody will push you. It'll just be hot – hot and close – for everyone.

VIOLET: I can remember working in places where you had to move like a ballet dancer, weave in and out of tables with grace. There was room, it was civilized.

KEVIN: Starch and clean finger-nails – I heard about it.

[HETTIE *goes off sniggering at* VIOLET.]

VIOLET [*to* HETTIE]: And we didn't mind either – we had to queue up and be inspected, all of us, chefs too – it was civilized. I once served the Prince of Wales. Look at me, bruises.

KEVIN: Look at her! Look at me, three stone lighter!

HANS [*to* KEVIN]: Marango will try to make you stay.

KEVIN: Now there's a man. Have you watched him? One of the girls dropped some cups by there this morning and he cried, 'me wages' he cried. 'All me wages down there!' And do take notice of the way he strolls among us all? I thought he'd a kind face, but when he's done talking with you his kindness evaporates. In thin air it goes, sudden, and his face gets worried as though today were the last day and he had to be closing for good and he were taking a last sad glance at everything going on. This mornin' he watched me a while, and then walked away shaking his head as though I were dying and there was not a drop of hope for me left an' all.

HANS [*to* PETER]: What he has said?

PETER: Marango spielt den lieben Gott!

[DAPHNE *wanders away but not before she takes a piece of cake from* PAUL.]

PAUL [*to* DAPHNE]: Bon appetit.

GASTON: Paul you got some cake?

PAUL [*to* RAYMOND]: Give the boy some cake. [*To* HANS.] You got over this morning yet?

HANS [*taking a cake* RAYMOND *is offering round*]: This morning, ach! He's a big fool, that Max. He's like a dustbin.

RAYMOND: So why you take notice? Look at them.

[MAX *and* NICHOLAS *are pointing at each other in some sort of argument, waving fingers, pulling faces and swaying.*]

NICHOLAS: No! No! No! I'm never going to listen to you again, never.

MAX: Good, very good. I'm fed up with you hanging around me anyway. 'Max should I do this, Max should I do that?' Well, Max isn't your father.

NICHOLAS: You're damn right he's not my father. My father was a man with kindness, my father never betray what I tell him.

MAX: Well *I* didn't betray what you told me either, I keep telling you –

NICHOLAS: My father brought up nine children and all of them good people –

MAX: I didn't tell anyone, I keep telling you –

NICHOLAS: My father –

MAX: Your father nothing! He's been dead since you was three years old so give that one a miss also.

RAYMOND: The first thing in the morning they come in and drink a bottle of beer. Then they're happy. All day they drink.

PAUL [*to* HANS]: What did Max say then exactly?

HANS: He doesn't like I talk in German [*Tragically.*] You know Paul you – you are a Jew and me – I'm German; we suffer together.

[PAUL *stiffens, relaxes, laughs ironically, hands* HANS *the red flower from his lapel.* HANS *returns to his station.*]

KEVIN [*to* HANS]: Is that a Jew then?

HANS [*sentimentally*]: A very good boy.

KEVIN: Well who'd have thought that, now.

[*At this point a* TRAMP *wanders into the kitchen. He is looking for the* CHEF. *Everyone stares at him and grins.*]

MAX [*shouting across to* BERTHA]: Bertha, ha, ha, is this your old man come after you? [*General laughter.*]

BERTHA: I'll come after you in a minute, pack it in.

[*The* TRAMP *comes over to the group of young men and talks to* KEVIN.]

TRAMP: 'Scuse me. The Chef please, which'n is he?

KEVIN: Napoleon there.

TRAMP: 'Scuse me, Chef [*touching his knee*], war disabled, I don't usually ask for food but I lost me pensions book see? I don't like to ask but . . .

CHEF: Michael, clean a tin and give him some soup.

TRAMP [*to* KEVIN]: Don't usually do this. Can't do anything till they trace me book. [*To* HANS.] Got it in the desert, 'gainst Rommel.

HANS: Rommel! Aha!

TRAMP: Got papers to prove it too. Here, look, papers! Always carry these around with me, everyone got to have his papers and I always carry mine. Be daft for the like 'o me to leave them anywhere, wouldn't it? Who'd believe me otherwise, see? Papers! Whatcha making? Spaghetti bolonaizeeee? That's good that Italian food. Do you put bay leaves in? Good with bay leaves, not the same without. Bay leaves, red peppers, all that stuff. What's this? [*Sees half-made arch.*] A castle? [*Sees dish-cloth, picks it up, and idly balances it on the tip of one of the handles, laughs and looks to see whether others are amused.* MICHAEL *hands him a tin of soup.*]

MICHAEL: Here you are.

TRAMP: Got a cigarette?

MICHAEL: Yes, and I'm smoking it.

MAX: Go on, 'op it, be quick, we got work.

PETER [*goes up to* TRAMP, *and looks in the tin; takes tin from* TRAMP *and offers it to* MAX]: You drink it?

MAX: Ah get out of it, you and your high and bloody mighty gestures. *I* work for my living. Fool!

> [PETER *ignores him and tosses the tin into the dustbin. Then he moves to* HAN's *station, and brings back two meat cutlets which he gives to the* TRAMP.]

PETER: Take these cutlets. [*Gently pushing him.*] Now go, quick, whist!

> [*But he is not quick enough. The* CHEF *approaches, and stands looking on.*]

CHEF [*quietly*]: What's that.

PETER: I gave him some cutlets.

CHEF: Mr Marango told you to give him?

PETER: No but . . .

CHEF: You heard me say, perhaps?

PETER: No, I . . .

CHEF: You have authority suddenly?

PETER [*impatiently*]: So what's a couple of cutlets, we going bankrupt or something?

CHEF: It's four and six that's what, and it's me who's Chef that's what and . . . [PETER *moves away muttering* 'ach'. *The* CHEF *follows him, annoyed now.*] Don't think we're too busy I can't sack you. Three years is nothing you know, you don't buy the place in three years, you hear me? You got that? Don't go thinking I won't sack you.

> [*By this time* MR MARANGO *appears on his round, hands in pocket.*]

MARANGO: Yes?

CHEF: The tramp – Peter gave him a cutlet, it was his own supper.

[CHEF *returns to his work, dispersing the crowd on the way.* MR MARANGO *simply nods his head at* PETER. *It is a sad nodding, as though* PETER *had just insulted him. He walks from right of stage to the left in a half circle round* PETER, *nodding his head all the time.*]

MARANGO [*softly*]: Sabotage. [*Pause.*] It's sabotage you do to me. [*Sadly taking his right hand out of his pocket, and waving it round the kitchen.*] It's my fortune here and you give it away. [*He moves off muttering* 'sabotage'.]

PETER: But it . . .

MARANGO: [*not even bothering to look round*]: Yes, yes, I'm always wrong – of course – yes, yes. [*Moves off into dining-room.*]

[*Everyone settles back into place.* PETER *goes to get a cup of coffee and makes faces at Marango's back, then he returns beside* ALFREDO. HANS *joins them.*]

HANS: Ou, pass auf, der ist wirklich hinter dir her!

PETER: Ach, er erwartet, dass die ganze Welt auf seine Küche aufpasst!

KEVIN: I seem to remember being told not to grumble by someone.

PETER: A bastard man. A bastard house.

KEVIN: And he also said you could get used to anything.

PETER: But this house is like – is like –

PAUL: Yeah? What is it like?

PETER: God in heaven, I don't know what it's like. If only it – if only it –

KEVIN: Yes, yes, we know all that – if only it would all go.

PETER: Just one morning – to find it gone.

PAUL: Fat lot of good you'd be if it went – you couldn't even cough up a dream when it was necessary.

PETER: A dream?

HANS: Ja, Pete, wo bleibt der Traum, den du uns versprochen hast?

PETER: I can't, I can't. [*Sadly.*] I can't dream in a kitchen! [*Violently kicks down other half of arch.*]

HANS: Aha! Und jetzt spielst du wieder den wilden Mann!

[*Enter* BERTHA *with a colander and* MONIQUE. *Both watch this.*]

BERTHA [*to* MONIQUE]: Why don't you hop it, out of here, girl like you –

MONIQUE: Girl like me *what*?

BERTHA: Pack it in, Monique. Peter I mean – dissolve it.

MONIQUE: Just like that?

BERTHA: Just like that.

MONIQUE: Just – like – that, huh! Twice he's given me a baby, twice I've disappointed him. He wanted them both. Dissolve that.

BERTHA: Aaaaah why don't we all hop it?

MONIQUE: Good question, Aunty Bertha.

PETER [*moving to* MONIQUE]: I'm sorry.

MONIQUE: Not an attractive future, is it? Apologizing backwards and forwards. First you, then me ...

PETER: Did you see that tramp?

MONIQUE: What tramp?

PETER: You didn't hear?

MONIQUE: Hear what?

PETER [*boasting and laughing, trying to pacify her*]: I had a row about him, Mr Marango and the Chef there, they wanted to give him a dirty tin full of soup so I threw it away and gave him some cutlets.

MONIQUE: And Marango caught you?

PETER [*imitating*]: 'Sabotage,' the old man said. 'Sabotage, all my fortune you take away.'

MONIQUE: Oh Peter!

PETER [*tenderly*]: Listen, do you want to know where I went this afternoon? To buy your birthday present.

MONIQUE: A present?

WINNIE [*to* HANS]: One veal cutlet.

WINNIE [*to* KEVIN]: Two plaice.

[PETER *takes out a necklace, and places it round her neck. She relents, turns to him, and pulls him to her, bites his neck.*]

CYNTHIA [*to* HANS]: One veal cutlet.

HANS: One veal cutlet. [*Long sad glance at her.*]

CYNTHIA [*to* MICHAEL]: One minestrone.

MICHAEL: One minestrone.

GWEN [*to* MICHAEL]: Minestrone.

PETER: Ah, you want to eat me. How do you want me? Grilled? Fried? Underdone? Well done?

[*While* PETER *and* MONIQUE *continue to talk affectionately, a sudden cry comes up from the back of the kitchen.* WINNIE *has doubled up in pain, and passed out. A crowd rushes to her – it all happens very quickly, hardly noticed. The boys at the table simply*

62

glance round and watch but do not move. PETER *and* MONIQUE *do not even hear it. We can only hear a few confused voices.*]

ALFREDO: All right, now don't crowd round, take her into the dining-room. Don't crowd round. [*Crowd disperses as* TRAMP *is taken into dining-room.*]

PAUL: Who was it? What's happened, then?

MOLLY: It's Winnie, she's passed out.

KEVIN: Well what was all that now?

GASTON: The heat. Always affecting someone. Terrible.

[*Meanwhile . . .*]

PETER [*to* MONIQUE]: Did you – er – you still going to do it. I mean I . . .

MONIQUE: Don't worry Peter, I shall see to it now. It's not the first time is it?

PETER: You don't think we should go through with it?

MONIQUE: I had a dream about blood last night.

PETER: I don't mind being responsible.

MONIQUE: I was in a slaughterhouse . . .

PETER: After all it is my baby.

MONIQUE . . . walking through it, like a roving camera's eye. There were men *and* women, all working on carcasses. The odd thing about the women was that they were all made up, beautifully groomed hair, carefully lipsticked and rouged and powdered. But splashed with blood. Blood. It was everywhere. The most horrifying moment was when I came across a group of slaughterers standing around a cow, and although the cow was skinned and had its eyes gouged out yet it was still alive and on its feet. Somehow I seemed to know that doing it this way improved the quality of the meat. And there was one man in particular, with a long stick at the end of which was a curved, very sharp knife, and he was slicing off the right-hand cheek of the cow's face. And the animal stood, shuddering, blind, passive.

PETER: The dream warns. You should have the b—

MONIQUE: Enough! I'm not going to talk about it any more.

PETER: You told Monty about us then?

MONIQUE: You really must stop rowing with Marango, darling.

PETER: Did you speak to Monty as we said?

MONIQUE: They won't stand it all the time, you know. I'm always telling you about this, Peter.

PETER: Listen Monique, I love you. Please listen to me that I love you. You said you love me but you don't say to your husband this thing.

HETTIE [*to* FRANK]: Two chicken.

MONIQUE: Now not this again.

PETER: You are not going to leave him are you? You don't really intend to?

MONIQUE: Oh Peter, please.

PETER: What do you want I should do then?

MONIQUE: Did the Chef say much?

PETER: We could leave any day. We could go for a long holiday first. Ski-ing in Switzerland perhaps.

MONIQUE: I am going to the hairdresser tomorrow as well.

PETER: Monique, we row this morning, we row in the afternoon too, this evening we are almost in love again . . . Answer me.

MONIQUE: Did I tell you Monty's going to buy me a house?

PETER [*screaming*]: Monique!

[MONIQUE *looks round in embarrassment and, muttering* 'You fool,' *stalks off*. VIOLET *approaches* PETER.]

VIOLET [*subdued – to* PETER]: You serving yet, Peter? I want three turbot. Special for Marango.

PETER: It's half past six yet?

VIOLET: It's nearly . . .

PETER: Half past six is service.

VIOLET: But it's special . . .

PETER: Half past six!

DAPHNE [*to* HANS]: Two sausages.

[*Service is just beginning. Evening service is not so hectic and takes a longer time to start up. Waitresses appear, most people are at their stations.*]

BETTY [*to* KEVIN]: Two plaice.

KEVIN: Me, I'd have a Jaguar. It's got a luxury I could live with.

GASTON: Have you seen the new French Citroën? Just like a mechanical frog it looks.

HANS: And the Volkswagen? It's not a good car?

KEVIN: Now there's a good little car for little money.

HANS: No country makes like the Volkswagen.

KEVIN: You've gotta hand it to the Germans.

[*More waitresses are coming in, but the service is easy and orders ring out in comfort.* CYNTHIA, *however, breaks her journey round the kitchen, and, with a glass of wine, goes up to the* CHEF *to gossip.* MAX *and* NICHOLAS *stand by listening.*]

CYNTHIA: Heard what happened to Winnie? She's been rushed to hospital.

MAX: What did she do wrong then?

CYNTHIA: She was pregnant.

MAX: She didn't look it.

CYNTHIA: I know. She didn't give herself a chance.

CHEF: Misfired?

CYNTHIA: I'll say, and it weren't no accident neither.

MAX [*shaking his head*]: Silly woman, silly woman.

CHEF: She's got seven children already, though.

CYNTHIA: That's right. Marango's hopping mad. It started happening on the spot, in there, in the dining-room. May and Sophie had to take her away.

MAX: What did she do, then?

CYNTHIA: She took pills, that's what. And I'll tell you something else, there are four other girls here took the same pills. There! Four of them!

BETTY [*to* HANS]: Two veal cutlets.

CYNTHIA: And you know who one of the four is? [*She inclines her head in Peter's direction.*]

MAX: Monique?

CYNTHIA [*nodding her head triumphantly*]: Now don't you tell anyone I told you, mind. But you ask Hettie, ask her, she bought the stuff. [*Continues on the round to* KEVIN.] Two plaice, please.

GWEN [*to* HANS]: Two hamburgers.

MAX: Knew this would happen.

HETTIE: Two halibut. [*This is said to* PETER, *who sits on stool centre, back to audience.*]

MAX: Knew it. Can't be done, though. What makes them think that by taking a tablet through the mouth it will affect the womb?

HETTIE: Oh come on Peter, two halibut.

[PETER *slowly rises to serve her.*]

MAX: There's only one way, the way it went in ... What happens with a tablet? Nothing ... Nothing can.

[PETER *serves only one halibut.*]

HETTIE [*to* PETER]: I said two.

MAX: The stomach is irritated, that's all, squeezed see? Forces the womb. Presses it.

NICHOLAS: Now what do you know about this? A doctor now?

MAX: Oh I know about this all right. Only one drug is effective through the mouth. [*Secretively*] And you know what that is? Ergot? Heard of it? Only thing to do it. And that's rare. Oh yes, I studied this in the forces when I had nothing else to do. Very interesting, this psychology. Complicated. I knew Winnie was in pod as soon as she came here.

[*All the time, the pastrycooks have been clearing away their station and are now ready to go. They are saying goodbye to everyone.* MAX *shouts to them as they go.*]

MAX: Some people have it easy!

[*The pastrycooks begin to leave, and, as they do so, an argument flares up suddenly at* PETER's *station.*]

MOLLY [*to* HANS]: Two sausages.

GWEN [*to* PETER]: One turbot.

DAPHNE [*to* PETER]: Three cod.

PETER: It's not ready yet.

DAPHNE: Oh come on Peter, three cod.

PETER: It's not ready yet, come back five minutes' time.

[*All the other chefs sing* 'Hi lee, hi lo, hi la' *at him.*]

MOLLY [*to* HANS]: Four veal cutlets.

GWEN [*to* PETER]: Six turbot.

JACKIE [*to* PETER]: Two halibut.

VIOLET [*to* PETER]: Two turbot. [*As there is a queue she tries to help herself.*]

PETER [*to* VIOLET]: You wait for me yes? *I* serve you. You ask *me*.

VIOLET: But you were busy.

PETER: I don't care. This is my place and there [*points to the side of bar*], there is for you.

VIOLET: Now you wait a bloody minute will you? Who the hell do you think you are, you?

PETER: You don't worry who I am. I'm the cook yes? And you're the waitress, and in the kitchen I do what I like yes? And in the dining-room you do what you like.

VIOLET [*taking another plate from off the oven*]: I won't take orders from you, you know, I . . .

PETER [*shouting and smashing the plate from her hand for a second time*]: Leave it! Leave it there! I'll serve you. Me! Me! Is *my* kingdom here. This is the side where *I* live. This.

VIOLET [*very quietly*]: You Boche you. You bloody German bastard!
[*She downs plates on the bar and walks off.* PETER *follows her. There is a general uproar and protest from the other waitresses who are waiting to be served.*]

PETER: What you call me? What was it? Say it again. [*He screams at her.*] SAY IT AGAIN! [*She halts, petrified.*]

[*The scream calls the attention of most people to him. They all stare at him as at a frightened animal. Suddenly he wheels round and in a frenzy searches for something violent to do. He rushes up to* VIOLET. *Seems about to attack her, but she is not the enemy. He knocks plates off one of the counters. Other chefs rush to hold him. He breaks away and reaches for a large chopper. Everyone backs away. Then with a cry of 'auf geht's,' he dashes to a part under a serving-counter and smashes something underneath. There is a slow hiss and all the fires of the ovens die down. There is a second of complete silence before anybody realizes what has happened, and then* FRANK *and two others are upon him, trying to hold him down. The* CHEF, *at last moved to do something, rushes to the scene, but* PETER *breaks away again and flees to the dining-room.* FRANK *and others follow. All this has happened too quickly for anyone to do a great deal about it, but in the scuffle the following cries were heard –*]

MICHAEL: He's broken the gas lead! Someone turn off the main!
[MANGOLIS *exits to do so.*]

FRANK: Hold him, grab hold of him!

KEVIN: Jesus Christ he'll murder her.

HANS: Sei nicht dumm! Beherrsch dich! Lass sie laufen!

[*When* PETER *has rushed into the dining-room, there is another silence as everybody waits to hear what will happen next. Some are not even sure what has already happened. Suddenly there is a tremendous crash of crockery and glass to the ground. There are screams, some waitresses come back into the kitchen from dining-room.*]

KEVIN: Holy mother o' Mary, he's gone berserk.

GASTON: The lunatic! He's swept all the plates off the table in there.

MICHAEL: He's ripped his hands.

KEVIN: I knew something like this would happen, now I just knew it.

[*The crowd by the entrance to the dining-room makes way as*

ALFREDO *and* HANS *bring* PETER *back.* PETER's *hands are covered in blood. Some smears have reached his face. He looks terribly exhausted. They bring him down stage.* MICHAEL *hurriedly finds a stool.*]

CHEF [*to* MICHAEL]: Phone an ambulance.

WAITRESS: Monique is doing that now.

[MONIQUE *pushes through the crowd. She is sobbing but she carries the medical box and a table-cloth.* ALFREDO *snatches the cloth from her and rips it up. She tries to dab some liquid on* PETER's *hands, he jumps and pushes her away. This is too much for her; she leaves it all and rushes away.* ALFREDO, *however, simply takes* PETER's *hands and ties them up.*]

PETER: It hurts, Christ it hurts.

ALFREDO: Shut up!

CHEF [*bending close to* PETER]: Fool! [*He straightens up, and finding nothing else to say for the moment, bends down to repeat again.*] Fool! [*Pause.*] So? What? The whole kitchen is stopped. Fool!

PETER [*to* ALFREDO]: Now he cares.

CHEF [*incredulous and furious*]: What do you mean, 'Now he cares'?

ALFREDO [*gently moving* CHEF *out of the way so that he might tie up* PETER's *hands*]: Leave him Chef, leave him now.

CHEF [*reaching* PETER *another way*]: What do you mean, 'Now he cares'? *You* have to make me care? Forty years and suddenly *you* have to make *me* care?

[*At this point the crowd breaks away to let* MARANGO *in. He surveys the damage.*]

MARANGO [*with terrible calm*]: You have stopped my whole world. [*Pause.*] Did you get permission from God? Did you? There – is – no – one – else! You know that? No ONE!

FRANK: All right, take it easy Marango. The boy is going, he's going. He's ill, don't upset yourself.

MARANGO [*turning to* FRANK *and making a gentle appeal*]: Why does everybody sabotage me, Frank? I give work, I pay well, yes? They eat what they want, don't they? I don't know what more to give a man. He works, he eats, I give him money. This is life, isn't it? I haven't made a mistake, have I? I live in the right world, don't I? [*To* PETER] And you've stopped this world. A shnip! A boy! You've stopped it. Well why? Maybe you can tell me something I don't know – just tell me. [*No answer.*] I want to learn something. [*To the kitchen*] Is there something I don't know? [PETER *rises and in pain moves off. When he reaches a point back centre stage* MARANGO *cries at him.*] BLOODY FOOL! [*Rushes round to him.*] What more do you want? What is there more, tell me? [*He shakes* PETER, *but gets no reply.* PETER *again tries to leave. Again* MARANGO *cries out.*] What is there more? [PETER *stops, turns in pain and sadness, shakes his head as if to say* – 'if you don't know, I cannot explain'. *And so he moves right off stage.* MARANGO *is left facing his staff, who stand around, almost accusingly, looking at him. And he asks again –*] What is there more? What is there more? What is there more?

The Four Seasons

The Four Seasons was first presented at the Belgrade Theatre, Coventry, in August 1965, with Alan Bates as Adam and Diane Cilento as Beatrice. It subsequently transferred to the Saville Theatre in London on 21 September.

The play was directed for Coventry by Henrik Hirsch and redirected for London by Arnold Wesker.

The sets were designed by Zybnek Kolar of the Army Theatre, Prague.

DEDICATED

to the romantic revolution
to Maria Rosa, Edmundo, Abelardo, Bertina
to the innocent revolution
to Fidel, Camilo, Che, Pepe
to the undergraduate revolutionaries
to Ingrid, Jose, Rebecca, Ugo
to the amateur administrators
to Mario, Calvert, Maria Elena, Fernando
to the soldiers who sing
    and the singers who guard
to Portocarrero, Milian, George, Chiki
to the sea by my window, the Sierra Maestra, the Varadero beach and
    the peso that is not worth a dollar
to Asenneh, Enky, Rine, Candela
to the glorious mess you've made for the children who read and the
    waiters who learn
to Haydee Santamaria, Mirian, Pablo, Teresa

not because of the slogans which soon no one will believe but
    because you've turned the barracks into schools

not because of the 'traitors' you've killed to the whine of righteous
    words
but because of the seeds of forgiveness I know you have

not because you would ever win if the big fight came
but because you are not afraid that you might lose

to Cuba

CHARACTERS

ADAM
BEATRICE

PART ONE

WINTER

Two middle-aged people enter a deserted house. They have cases of belongings with them.

The house is furnished with a mixture of antiques which, if they have any beauty, have only the beauty that accompanies neglected and sad things; and of plain furniture assembled, perhaps, by hand.

It is evening. His name is ADAM, *her name is* BEATRICE.

They could be between thirty and forty years old.

ADAM: We're safe, it's all right, no one lives here. You don't think anywhere is safe do you?

My uncle's. Retired judge. Found nature too sad. Imagine fleeing this!

Won't you even say you like it? Say 'I like it'. Just those three words. Or 'I don't like it' or 'Let's leave'. Or give a deep sigh or smile. Won't you even sit down? You will if I bring you a chair won't you? I can see you'll do nothing unless I prepare it for you.

Right, then for the first weeks I'll prepare everything for you. Make your food, your bed, warm you. Just for the first weeks.

Try. Please. Say 'I – [*he waits*] like [*he waits*] it.'

Won't you even say three words?

[*No response.*]

Sit then. [*He pulls out a chair, dusts it, and gently leads her to sit down.*] Listen to that wind. Are you cold? I must put a new pane in that window tomorrow, or sometime. It *is* cold. [*He looks around for an object to stuff in the empty frame. An old piece of sacking serves the purpose. Then he rummages in his case and draws out two blankets.*] Here. Warm. The first thing, always, is to be warm. [*He places one over her legs.*] Invalid. You *are* an invalid aren't you? You're beautiful also.

[BEATRICE *closes her eyes, and sleeps.* ADAM *watches her for a long while.*

He raises his hand and is about to touch her face.]

No, I won't touch you. I wonder why sad faces are such lovely faces? Sleep, I won't touch you. [*Begins to unpack.*]

Such a lovely face. A face I could love. Even 'love' again. But I won't, lovely lady. Not love again. Not all that again. I'll give you human warmth but not human love. Not that again. Not all those old, familiar patterns of betrayal, those reproaches. And you know them, don't you? I can tell as you sleep, from the lines round your eyes, you know them.

What would you say if you were awake just now? You'd say 'Are you afraid? Are you afraid of love?' And I'd say 'Yes, I *am* afraid of love.' And you'd chide me, call me coward. 'Those who are afraid to die, die a thousand times,' you'd say. And then I'd feel mean for holding back and I'd give. Give and give and give because every part of me aches to give.

No. Not again. Not all that again.

[BEATRICE *wakes with a start.*]

Bad dreams? They'll pass. I'll get wood for a fire. [*He moves, then turns back.*] Won't you say three words, just three?

[*She remains silent and he leaves to gather some fuel.*
She watches him to the door and for a long time stares after him.
Soon her head moves back again to look at the room. Its sadness, its desolation, its cold reach into her. She is crying.
Her blanket falls to the ground and she slides from the chair to her knees, hugging the blanket to her.
ADAM *returns and stands by the door. He makes no move towards her. Sternly –*]

Get up. Beatrice, get up. Beatrice? Beatrice?

[*Slowly she returns to the chair. He moves to pick up the blanket and again lays it over her legs.*]

'Ye hasten to the dead? What seek ye there?' Do you know those lines? Shelley. 'Ye hasten to the dead? What seek ye there?' [*Now he lays the fire and lights it.*] Do you know I hardly know the sound of your voice? Is it shrill? Mellow? Thin? I used to sit in buses or trains and gaze at beautiful girls, and sometimes they'd smile at me and I'd smile back and imagine every virtue in their faces: gentleness, understanding, passion – and then they'd speak, and everything I'd imagined about them would shatter. How can lovely eyes have ugly voices I wonder? Is your soul on your lips or in your eyes? Answer me that. Just that. Say 'eyes' or 'lips', say. Or point.

Do that, even. Just point. Not even that?

Listen to the wood crackling. Smell it?

[*She breathes in, slowly, slightly.*]

Again, Beatrice, again.

[*Again she breathes in, this time a deeper breath.*]

Again, can you do it again?

[*She turns her head away; for his foolish persistence she has, for the moment, dismissed him.*]

You think I don't understand, don't you? How I recognize that look. The female dismissing the male. But can't you see pain in *my* eyes? Do you imagine I'd bring you here, commit a whole year to you if I understood nothing? Do you?

[*Pause.*]

Look, even the gas is on. [*He turns on a stove.*] Isn't it miraculous? [*He moves out of sight.*] AND THE WATER TOO. [*Sound of water; he returns.*] We've got fire and water. [*He picks up the other blanket and moves to a chair in which he sits, covering his legs, like her, and gazes at her.*] Isn't it miraculous?

[*There is a long pause as the two sit. The days are passing, the weeks, even.*]

[ADAM *rises abruptly from the chair and throws his blanket down. It is morning.*]

ADAM: Gentleness is no good, I can see that. It just produces more self-pity doesn't it? [*He busies himself with putting the room to order, wiping away dust and cobwebs.*] Look at you. Call yourself a woman? Your face is falling apart with self-pity. You don't impress me with your silence. I could do that, what you're doing, sitting there, silent, morbid, lifeless. I could do that. You're even enjoying it aren't you? How lovely it is, suffering. All the world is against you isn't it? Eh? All the world is a fool, and you're alone and suffering. [*Mockingly*] 'I'm alone. I'm born alone. We're all, all born alone.' Lovely. Splendid. Very satisfying. Suffering. Lovely, lovely suffering.

And yet I know. Why should I mock you? I know.

You were right to dismiss me, we don't really know each other, yet. Poor girl, we grieve for our*selves* don't we?

But look, I live! I go on, Beatrice, I go on.

You don't believe me do you? She doesn't believe me. [*Writes*

77

this in the dust on a piece of furniture.] She – doesn't – believe – me.
[*He pretends to hear this next question from someone far off, cupping
his ears.*] Eh? What's that? Why doesn't she believe me? Why?
[*Shouts back answer.*] BECAUSE YOU NEVER RECOVER, NEVER.
That's why.

Why don't we ever recover, Beatrice? Won't you answer that even?

Not even that you'll answer. Poor Beatrice. I mean that; poor,
poor Beatrice. 'Poor Adam' do I hear you say? [*He moves to the
window, listlessly surveying the bleak outside.*] What colour is the
wind, do you think?

Perhaps we should wait for the winter to pass.

[*They are really living in their own hells.
The days are passing, the weeks, even.*]

[ADAM *sings to her. It is late evening.*]

ADAM: 'The wind doth blow tonight my love,
               And a few small drops of rain:
               I never had but one true love,
               In cold grave she was lain.

[*He recites the rest.*]
               I'll do as much for my true love
               As any young man may;
               I'll sit and mourn all at her grave
               For a twelvemonth and a day.'

See. even *I* have become morbid. If we stay together many more
months, do you think we'll just fall apart? Disintegrate with
misery? Waste away? Look, if I stand here, by the window, and
you sit there, day after day, quite still, do you think God would
take pity on us and turn us to stone for ever and ever? Let's try.
You, there, me, here. Quite still. Don't move now.

[*They freeze for a long time. Then –*]

Have you ever known a God as unobliging as yours?

[BEATRICE *smiles.* ADAM *moves quickly to face her.*]

You smiled. I caught you smiling, don't deny it. For that – a
present. Today a special treat.

[ADAM *moves quickly to his case and withdraws a hairbrush. Then
he stands behind* BEATRICE *and takes the pins from her hair till a
lovely mane falls behind her.
He brushes with caressing firmness.*]

78

See what we give to the people we comfort? The tested gestures of love! Those very things that we know have given pleasure to others before. Does that offend you? But what's the alternative? Immobility? Silence? I used to remain silent because it seemed to me that all my thoughts should be kept for one person only. To know more than one person was to betray them, I thought. You know, it was my silence – more than anything else – that made my wife miserable. That, more than anything else. But what could I say? What could I tell her? Every ounce of passion was claimed, given elsewhere.

But she had her retribution, my wife. One day a young man came from another country to be our guest. He had eyes like an uncertain child in a strange and festive room and he laughed with pleasure at everything he saw. And gradually I watched my wife unfold from her misery as she gathered the tested gestures of *our* love, and revealed all the secret corners of *our* tested past. And he held her hand and blessed her kindness as they walked over bridges and looked into rivers and ate in our friendly restaurants. For two weeks she blossomed as she once did. Every ounce of *her* passion was now claimed, given elsewhere. And as I lay in bed till the early hours, waiting for her return, no one at my side, imagining the tenderness and passions they were sharing then, just then, at that precise and very moment – I clenched my teeth and cried 'justice' to myself. Justice, justice, justice! [*Pause*] To know more than one person *is* to betray them.

But who remains silent for ever?

You have lovely hair. [*He moves to kneel in front of her.*] Beatrice, you have lovely hands, and eyes, and lips and skin. Do you forgive me for saying it? You don't know what it means to be able to say those things to a woman. You only know that a woman needs to hear them said but you don't know the pain that grows in a man who is struck dumb with no one to say them to, you don't know that do you? No, I won't touch you, but will you let me look at you?

Do you think the winter will ever pass?

[*He lays his head in her lap, fatigued. His eyes close, he breathes deeply. She regards him for some seconds, then slowly raises her hand to stroke his head. It has cost her to do this and after the effort her body relaxes. She too closes her eyes. The night passes, the days, the weeks, even. Till –*]

SPRING

A long ray of sunshine cuts through the room. It is morning.
BEATRICE *opens her eyes.*
At first she is startled, then she realizes where she is. Very gently she raises ADAM's *head, takes her blanket to cushion him where her lap was, slides off her chair and moves out of the house.*
In her absence the sunlight grows stronger and the room is witness to winter passing.
She returns, in her hands a large bunch of bluebells. These she lays upon the still-sleeping ADAM *till he is decorated from head to foot. On the last flower he awakes.*

ADAM: Woken with flowers? Not since –
BEATRICE: See what we give to the people we comfort? The tested gestures of love.
ADAM: You woke your lover with bluebells?
BEATRICE: Every morning.
ADAM: And at night?
BEATRICE: Oiled my skin with a different scent.
ADAM: Lucky man.
BEATRICE: Lucky? Loved!
ADAM: Some women make their lovers wait and offer love as though it were a favour.
BEATRICE: Your sluts and your whores do that, but not your women, not your real women.
ADAM: Then you're a rare woman.

    Now what is it? Your face has fallen again.
BEATRICE: Too many people have considered me a rare woman.
ADAM: But aren't you? You seem so sure, so confident, even your silence was confident. Look at you. Proud head, penetrating eyes – too penetrating perhaps, but sad also, and weary. Haunting, and weary.
BEATRICE: Aren't you intimidated?
ADAM (*teasing*): But of course! I feel I want to rush away and change my clothes, they're all wrong and ill-shaped. The clothes I have belong to a city-clerk or an estate agent, they should belong to a prince. The brush I brushed your hair with is made of nylon, it should be made of bristle. And the way you hold your head and

glance at me makes me feel clumsy and careless. Of course I'm intimidated, but what should I do – you *are* a rare woman.

There, your face has fallen again. Is it something I've said? Are we going to return to silence again? It *is* something I've said, isn't it?

BEATRICE: You must not –

ADAM: Must not what?

BEATRICE: You must not –

ADAM: What? What? What must I not?

BEATRICE: Gently, Adam, gently. You must allow me –

ADAM: – all the world! All the world I'll allow you. How can I refuse you? Look at the sun, look at that morning, it's a morning for offerings. All the world I'll offer you, only ask. Just ask.

My mother used to ask me, 'Do you love me?' and I'd say 'Yes!' And then she'd say, 'How much?' and I'd say 'Sixpence' and she'd say 'Is that all?' And I'd say 'Two and sixpence.' 'No more?' she'd ask. And I'd say, 'All the world then. I love you all the world all the world all the world all the world.'

What more can I offer you? Fourpence for a cup of tea? The cream off the milk? They're yours, and the sun and this whole morning.

BEATRICE: You'll drown me with your words.

ADAM: I embarrass you?

BEATRICE: No.

ADAM: Overwhelm you?

BEATRICE: No.

ADAM: Then thank God for me and stop complaining – that's the way I feel. After a winter of silence that's the way I feel. Stop complaining.

[*There is a terrible sound of crashing from outside.* ADAM *goes to see what has happened. Soon he returns with a fallen drainpipe, and some broken tree-branches.*]

ADAM: Spring comes and it's time to repair the damages of winter.

[*He looks round the room and, on seeing a broken hatstand, places the drainpipe over it and puts the branches into the drainpipe. There is now a 'tree' in the room which, when the walls later move aside, becomes a tree in the country scene.*]

Are you fit?

BEATRICE (*playfully*): Your command is my wish.

ADAM: I see. It's to be like that is it? I'm always suspicious of a woman's offer of obedience. Still, I'll risk it, even again. You want me to give the orders? I'll give them. First of all – food. Prepare food. Can you cook?

BEATRICE: I can try. [*She goes to the stove and shows him the inside.*] Will this do?

ADAM: It smells of Italy. You *can* cook.

BEATRICE: Why should you imagine I can't cook, or run a household? You mistake my silence for inability.

ADAM: You're cheating. Obedience and false modesties – there's no time.

BEATRICE: Come now, if I have false modesties you have false innocence.

ADAM: Aaaaaah!

BEATRICE: Did that hurt?

ADAM: Didn't you mean it to hurt?

BEATRICE: I'm sorry. Old reflexes.

ADAM: But it came so easily, so quickly.

BEATRICE: I've developed the habit. I'm sorry.

ADAM: You put me on guard.

BEATRICE: Please – don't be on guard.

[ADAM *relents and prepares the table with a great flourish.*
A splendid white cloth is produced and cutlery and crockery drawn out from the sideboard.]

ADAM: I'm ravenous. I could eat a hundred sheep and drink a hundred tankards of beer.

BEATRICE: I'm afraid the village didn't have much of a selection of wines, there was only this.

ADAM: Stop apologizing.

BEATRICE: And these, look, there was a little antique shop, I picked them up cheaply.

ADAM: Serviette rings! We're building a home! Silver?

BEATRICE: Georgian too.

ADAM: You know?

BEATRICE: Quite cheap, I promise you. The poor man didn't really know what they were.

ADAM: So of course you had to buy the serviettes.

BEATRICE: Are you angry?

ADAM: Angry?

BEATRICE: At my extravagance?

ADAM: Stop apologizing. We're building a home. White linen! It'll be a royal meal.

BEATRICE: And forgive me, this material, I thought I'd make a dress. Golden for the summer.

ADAM: It's beautiful.

BEATRICE: And I found this pullover also. I thought it might suit you. Do you like it? You don't think it presumptuous? I'm sorry if you –

ADAM: Please, please, I can't bear you being apologetic all the time. You knew it would suit me.

BEATRICE: I'm not always sure about people, not everyone likes things chosen for them.

ADAM: Not everyone likes another's choice to be so right.

[*Pause.*]

What colour shall we paint these walls?

BEATRICE: White.

ADAM: And what should be the colour of the curtains?

BEATRICE: Golden.

ADAM: And the covering of the furniture?

BEATRICE: Golden again.

ADAM: You're so sure. You answer so quickly.

BEATRICE: A minor accomplishment.

ADAM: Thank you. [*He moves to kiss her.*] No, I won't touch you. Won't you sit, ma'am?

[ADAM *ceremoniously pulls out a chair for her, uncorks the wine and pours their drinks. Then he takes his seat at the other end of a long table.*]

ADAM: To whom, or what, shall we drink?

BEATRICE: Perhaps we should just raise our glasses and not tempt fate.

ADAM: Are you still afraid?

BEATRICE: Afraid? I'm neither afraid nor brave. I feel nothing. Let's just drink.

[*They raise glasses to each other and drink, slowly, remaining still when the glasses are drained.*]

BEATRICE: Do you know what my husband once said to me? 'You're like a queen,' he said, 'without a country. I hate queens without their country.' *He* felt nothing and *I* felt nothing. We spent the last years living a cold courteous lie.

ADAM: But your lover?

BEATRICE: He was a leader of men.

ADAM: He was or you wanted him to be?

BEATRICE: That's just what he would have asked.

ADAM: Ah ha! Then I know him and I know you and I know all that passed between you.

Now you look tragic.

BEATRICE: Neither tragic nor glad. I'm indifferent.

[BEATRICE *fills her glass and drinks alone. They sit in silence. Her indifference turns to anger*.]

That! That more than anything else is what I can't forgive. They made me feel indifference. I can't bear indifference. I despise the man who dares to make me feel indifference, despise him.

ADAM: Beatrice –

BEATRICE: From my husband I expected no more, but from him –

ADAM: You're not talking to *me*, Beatrice.

BEATRICE: From him – to spit at the devotion I chose to give him.

ADAM: You're not talking to *me*.

BEATRICE: He'll find no one, no one to give him so much.

ADAM: BEATRICE!

BEATRICE: No matter where he searches or for how long, no one!

[ADAM *rises and begins clearing away*.]

BEATRICE: I'm sorry.

ADAM: I've bought some paint, we must paint the house.

BEATRICE: Forgive me.

ADAM: From top to bottom. We must paint the house from top to bottom if we intend to live the year out together.

BEATRICE: You're so gentle, I didn't mean to hurt you, forgive me.

ADAM: We'll greet the spring with those white walls.

BEATRICE: I don't ever mean to hurt anyone, forgive me.

ADAM: We'll greet the spring with white walls and the summer with golden curtains.

BEATRICE: I'll look in the shops for bits and pieces, I'll make them myself.

ADAM: What more can I do? I don't know what more I can do. Everything explodes.

BEATRICE: I promise, I promise.

ADAM: I have a desperate need to give joy, to make someone laugh, to heal, not destroy. To heal, to heal.

BEATRICE: And I need to be healed. I've destroyed a marriage and failed a lover – I need to be healed.

ADAM: O ye gods! How we go on. We must stop this – encouraging each other's misery. Let's see how long we can stay away from morbidity.

Can you use a paintbrush?

BEATRICE: I can try, my lord.

ADAM: Am I your lord?

BEATRICE: You are.

ADAM: Really, really your lord?

BEATRICE: Really, really.

ADAM: Then take this brush. [*He brings in brushes and a pail of whitewash from the kitchen; also two white aprons.*] And wear this.

[*They dress themselves in whites, take up a brush and then turn, each a different way, looking for the wall to start on first.*]

This one?

BEATRICE: No, that one.

ADAM [*after the merest pause*]: That one, then.

[*They attack the wall.*]

> 'When I was a windy boy and a bit
> And the black spit of the chapel fold,'

BEATRICE: You recite.

ADAM: 'Sighed the old ram rod, dying of women,'

BEATRICE: You sing.

ADAM: 'I tiptoed shy in the gooseberry wood,
> The rude owl cried like a telltale tit,
> I skipped in a blush as the big girls rolled
> Ninepin down on the donkey's common
> And on seesaw Sunday nights I wooed
> Whoever I would with my wicked eyes . . .'

BEATRICE: What else do you do?

ADAM: I dance.

BEATRICE: And?

ADAM: And I weave tapestries.

BEATRICE: Large ones?

ADAM: Vast and intricate.

BEATRICE: Full of fantasies?

ADAM: Yes, but how did you know?

BEATRICE: How much I know about you already.

ADAM: And you?

BEATRICE: I? Oh, none of those things. Men come to me with their ideas, politicians with their doubts, poets ask my praise. My home is filled with people seeking comfort because they know my instinct is right. Which woman for the right man, the correct meal for a gathering, the strength of an argument. But for myself? In my little finger is all the energy and the taste to shape so much, and yet I flutter from one grand scheme to the next and settle my mind nowhere.

ADAM: Sing, you must be able to sing.

BEATRICE: Not even that. I thought I could, till my voice rasped back at me through a tape recorder. Somehow I can't seem to make the notes happen. A sort of moan comes out, a gurgle, a sort of gasping for air.

ADAM: Now that I find sad. I don't believe you. Everybody can sing, I've never heard of anyone not being able to sing. Why it must have been the first sound of the first man.

BEATRICE: It wasn't you know. The first man gave a long wail and ran round and round in terror. It must have been the most nerve-racking shock in the world at that moment. There was his wife and there were his children – and he ran, a long, long way away. He ran.

ADAM: Wrong! It wasn't a wail of terror at all, it was a cry of joy, a great leap in the air. And it only seemed as though he ran a long way because he got lost in all the excitement.

BEATRICE [through her smile]: You don't really believe that do you, Adam?

ADAM: If I teach you to sing will you believe me?

BEATRICE: It just isn't possible, I know.

ADAM: If I give your throat a dozen notes will you believe me?

BEATRICE: You're very sweet, but –

ADAM: Will you?

BEATRICE: I –

ADAM: Will you?

    [*She is resigned.*

    He hums a melodic scale.]

    Try that.

    [*A dry, awful complaint comes from her throat.*]

BEATRICE: I must be mad. Adam, believe me. I feel embarrassed.

ADAM: You didn't listen. To have produced a sound like that you couldn't have listened.

BEATRICE: I listened, believe me, I heard you but I just couldn't repeat it, I heard you.

ADAM: Again. [*Again he hums the same scale.*]

BEATRICE: Please don't make me.

ADAM: Again.

[*He hums.*
She tries, and again a strange guttural sound comes from her throat.]

But you're not listening – everybody sings.

BEATRICE: I'll cry, if you go on I'll cry.

ADAM: It's like not having eyes, or being lame. What do you do with babies if you can't lullaby them? What sound do you make when you smell the first flowers?

BEATRICE: I can't, I can't, that's it. I can't. No sound, I make no sounds, just a long moan, or a silence. I destroyed a marriage and failed a lover, now leave me alone, damn you, leave me alone.

ADAM: Hush then, I'm sorry.

BEATRICE: Well I can't, I just can't sing.

ADAM: I'm sorry.

BEATRICE: I never could.

ADAM: Hush.

BEATRICE: You think I haven't tried? I've tried and I've tried, I just can't.

ADAM: I'm sorry.

My God, is there nothing we can touch that doesn't explode?

BEATRICE: Nothing.

There was nothing he or I could touch either that didn't explode. What battles we fought. I thought I saw 'God' in him but we fought. The 'boy with wings'. I used to sit at his feet, literally, curled on the floor, hugging him. 'Get up,' he'd say, he hated it, 'get up, off your knees, no woman should be on her knees to a man.' He never believed he was worth such devotion, it embarrassed him.

And I was dead, a piece of nothing until he touched me, or spoke to me, or looked at me. Even his look was an embrace. I used to nag him for all his thoughts, hungry for everything that passed through his mind, jealous that he might be thinking something he didn't want to share with me. I couldn't take my eyes off him. I knew every curve and movement his features made; I don't know why we fought.

That's a lie. I knew very well why we fought. I couldn't bear to see the shadow of another person fall on him. Even hearing him talk to someone else on the phone about 'ways to mend the world' was enough to make prickles of the hair on my neck. How dared he think my intellect was not enough to set to right his silly world's intolerable pain! Do you know what I used to do? Oh we're awful creatures all right; sneer, I used to sneer and denigrate anyone who was near and dear to him – friends, relatives, colleagues. Even his children. I couldn't bear the demands they made on him. When they were desperately ill I dismissed their complaints as childish maladies, and when they cried because their father constantly stayed away I accused them of artfulness. No one missed the whip of my sneers.

But he was a leader of men and leaders of men fight back. Every word became a sword, a giant bomb destroying nerve centres, crippling the heart. We hurled anything at each other: truth, lies, half-truths – what did it matter, as long as it was poison, as long as we gave each other no peace. Sometimes he'd give in, for love of me, and when the next battle came round I'd taunt him with his previous surrender, and when he didn't surrender I'd accuse him of being afraid of his wife. No peace, none at all, neither for him or myself.

Human communication difficult? Not for us it wasn't. We communicated only too well, he and I. In the end – we were demented, mad and demented. And for what? A love so desperate that we fought for it not to be recognized, terrified that we might reveal to each other how helpless we were. Isn't that madness? That's madness for you. Since without love I've neither appetite nor desire, I'm capable of nothing and I haven't the strength to forgive myself.

There, can you still teach me to sing? Teach me to love myself better – then perhaps I'll sing.

[ADAM *returns to the painting.*

BEATRICE *watches him.*]

How patient you are.

[*She also takes up painting again and both continue in silence.*

88

Softly ADAM *begins to sing the song he sang her in winter.*
BEATRICE *struggles to join him. Both are desperately trying to break her tenseness. Soon, they hum together, she slightly off key.*
ADAM *moves towards her, encouraging her.*]

Close your eyes.

[*He stops at once and obeys,* BEATRICE *rises, moves towards him, and for the first time touches him — her cheek to his, then body to body. There is no passionate embrace but there is passion.*]

Nothing should be held back, ever. I believe that, O Adam I believe that. We're mean, we're all so mean, nothing should be held back.

[*He holds her away from him to look at her face. She turns her face away from him.*]

ADAM: You're blushing.

BEATRICE: Don't look at me.

ADAM: Like a young girl, you're blushing.

BEATRICE: Please, just hold me, don't look at me.

ADAM: Why, why? I want to look at you. Lift your head, Beatrice, look at me. Don't turn away, look at me. Face me, face me.

[*She falls to her knees and buries her face in his limbs.*]

Wait.

[*He leaves her on her knees, clasping herself to herself, and goes to a drawer from which he takes her golden material. This he lays over her shoulders and raises her to her feet.*]

'Get up, off your knees, no woman should be on her knees to a man!' What about that golden dress, before the summer comes?

[BEATRICE *leaves, shrouded in her yellow cloth.*
When she is gone he collects brushes and paint, calling to her as he tidies.]

We'll paint ourselves a white temple. Do you hear that? A white temple! I'll worship you in it. Do you hear? A white temple to worship you in.

[*A white light burns the scene.*
The days have passed, the weeks, even.]

PART TWO

SUMMER

BEATRICE *enters.*

It is a new morning and, beautifully dressed in her yellow garment, she approaches the room, the day, the sun as though for the first time.

All is changed, white walls, the furniture newly covered in material matching the dress; and curtains – also golden – deck the windows.

She is in love with the room, the morning and herself. She stands before a mirror and stretches her limbs long and sensuously; then, embarrassed, she turns away and giggles to herself. In this mood she wanders round the room touching its many textures.

ADAM *enters and watches her for some seconds before she turns to him. They approach each other, and now, not for the first time, but remembering, she feels the shape of his body.*

He is about to speak but she gestures him not to. She does not want to talk, only to look at him, and this she does with a sort of incredulity, as though she cannot believe her good fortune. She pulls him gently round the room in order to see him in different lights. At times she moves a long way away from him and wanders round the room, at a great distance, as though to approach him would make him disappear. Every so often she turns her back on him and then turns swiftly back as though imagining he might be gone, as though tempting fate to take him.

When they are at such a distance, suddenly, the furniture and the walls of the room fly away. The 'tree' is there; the sun is yellow; they are out in the fields.

BEATRICE, *like a young girl, tucks her dress into her pants while* ADAM *bends to touch his toes and she, with a great 'whoop', runs and leaps over his back. Then he leaps over her.*

Now they just walk and walk, breathing the air, touching their finger tips, each stretching, each feeling the shape of their own bodies.

Soon they lie down, by a bank, under a tree, near a rick.

ADAM: Look at that bird, that one there, the one that just seems to be hanging in the air – do you believe it?

BEATRICE: Believe it?

ADAM: Believe in it.

BEATRICE: In its existence?

ADAM: No, no. Not its existence; I mean, well look at it. You can't really believe that it can stay in the air, just by flapping about like that, can you? Or can you? I suppose you can.

BEATRICE: What keeps it in the air then?

ADAM: God knows! Lots of other birds blowing up I think! And aeroplanes, all that metal in the air. All that metal and all those people stuck in the air, with nothing underneath them.

BEATRICE: Except air.

ADAM: Except air.

BEATRICE: And friends blowing up!

ADAM: – And ships! Silly isn't it? That mass of iron and wood –

BEATRICE: – and people –

ADAM: – and people, all floating –

BEATRICE: – with nothing under them –

ADAM: – except frogmen. Thousands of them. Swimming with one arm and holding up the boat with the other.

BEATRICE: And clouds.

ADAM: Clouds?

BEATRICE: Making all that noise, thunder – at least so they say.

ADAM: Oh that one. I've never believed that one.

BEATRICE: I mean what's a cloud? Mist! Nothing!

ADAM: And those flowers.

BEATRICE: Which ones?

ADAM: Those, over there, with all those colours and patterns – you know what they say about those don't you?

BEATRICE: What?

ADAM: That they – you won't believe this – that they come from a tiny seed, no bigger than this. All those colours, look! No bigger than this.

BEATRICE: They tried to tell me that one at school.

ADAM: Did you believe them?

[*Pause.*]

BEATRICE: I planted forests, once, in a remote part of the Highlands, for two years, reclaiming lost land. My father studied plants and I learned from him the drama of watching things grow. And when my university days were over I took to the hills and bandaged dying firs and damaged pines.

Have you ever heard of the *Soldanella* or the Shasta Daisy? The White Laurustinus and the Red Ice Plant? Did you know that *Convallaria majalis* was the Latin name for lily of the valley? 'Consider the *Convallaria majalis* how they grow, they toil not, neither do they spin; and yet . . .'

I made things grow, Adam, once I made things grow.

ADAM: And now?

BEATRICE: Now? [*Whispering mischievously in his ear*] I have a golden eagle for a lover.

ADAM: But the sun has burnt his wings.

BEATRICE: Nothing shall burn your wings – I am your sun.

ADAM: Where shall I fly?

BEATRICE: Anywhere – as long as you carry me with you.

ADAM: But aren't you my sun?

BEATRICE: When you need me to be your sun, I'm your sun. When you need comfort I'll offer my words. When you need rest I'll offer my breasts and my lips. Whatever you call for you shall have.

ADAM: And you? What shall I give you?

BEATRICE: Every second! Every touch, every thought, every feeling, every second shall thou givest me. [*She is testing him.*]

ADAM: 'Shall?' You demand?

BEATRICE: Do you deny me the right to demand?

ADAM [*long pause – then*]: I deny you nothing.

BEATRICE [*leaping up*]: I HAVE A GOLDEN EAGLE FOR A LOVER! [*Runs, cups her mouth, cries out.*] A GOLDEN EAGLE! [*Runs to another point, cups her mouth, cries out.*] I HAVE A GOLDEN EAGLE FOR A LOVER! Adam, are we ready? Are we ready now? Let's go now. Let's test ourselves away from here. Before the winter comes let's get away from this house, now. Now is the loveliest time, let's go –

ADAM: Now?

BEATRICE: Now, now! If we stay on we'll tempt fate.

ADAM: Not yet. Trust me.

BEATRICE: Don't you see what's happened to me? Dear God! I believe in everything. I'd like to be young again for you; I'd like to be shy and pure and untouched for you. Let's go, Adam. We've had this place, this time – we've had it, all it can give. There's nothing more here. Let's go.

ADAM: Trust me.

BEATRICE: Trust you? Oh I trust everything to you. I could tear myself apart for you, I could fly for you. I'm a flower, Adam see me? See me opening, watch me, I'm blossoming, watch me, watch meeeee.

> [BEATRICE *towers and slowly stretches out to the sun. The movement of her body matches the words she cries.*
> *She faces the sun.*
> ADAM *watches her turn to the sun and place her back to him.*
> *He turns and moves away from her.*
> *They freeze in this position.*
> *The sun sets.*
> *The walls and furniture return.*
> *The days are passing, the weeks, even.*]

ADAM: There are two kinds of love and two kinds of women. The woman whose love is around you, keeping its distance lest the heat of it burns you; and out of that warmth you emerge, slowly, confidently, as sure as the seed in her womb. And the woman whose love is an oppressive sun burning the air around you till you can't breathe and drying every drop of moisture from your lips till you can't speak; and she has a passion no part of which relates to any living man nor any living man could share.

You know, when I was born I was born with a great laughter in me. Can you believe that? A great laughter, like a blessing. And some people loved and some hated it. It was a sort of challenge, a test against which people measured themselves as human beings; and I could never understand, not at all, the extremes of their love or their hatred. Have you ever been with a beautiful woman, a really breathtaking beauty, and watched or felt the passionate waves of devotion and loathing she attracts, and noticed how the people around feel the irresistible need to say sly, unpleasant things to show they're not intimidated by her beauty? So it was with my laughter.

And she, who had no need to measure herself against anything or anyone because she was endowed with her own loveliness, her own intelligence – she too began to measure herself against that laughter. And why? Because it belonged to me you see; I was born with it, she couldn't bear that it hadn't been bestowed by her and so she began to measure herself against me and challenge all that was mine.

She found enemies where there were none and saw betrayals in every act. She broke each smile and stormed every moment of peace we had built. And once, when I wrote to her from a sick bed and cursed her, when *I* lost control, she perversely became calm and took control as if to show that she controlled my laughter, and only she could nurse me back to health. 'You,' she said, 'are incapable.'

Soon, there was no sense to her words. 'I see God in you,' she'd say one day and the next pour sourness on my work. She'd rave and regret, applaud and destroy, love and devour. Mad! Mad, mad, mad woman.

Why does a woman destroy her love with such a desperate possessiveness, why? She had no need to be desperate – I *was* possessed.

Where is she now, I wonder? [*Shrugs.*] Lonely. Lost somewhere and lonely. No one has the right to take away laughter from a man, or deny a woman her beauty. Lonely. Unutterably lonely.

And yet, despite what she is, there's a part of her that doesn't deserve what she is; I always understood. Through all that madness – and it is a madness you know, love like that, a madness – but through it all I understood her need to howl at the pain of such a tortuous relationship. And she knew, understood. In moments of peace we both understood and comforted each other. But then she'd forget and she'd howl again and I could never forgive her that her howl carried such terror, that her wounds spilt not clear blood but a venomous poison and that it went on and on and on and on, relentlessly, crippling us both. Dear God, she deserves her loneliness.

And I? I rummage about the world looking for bits and pieces of old passions, past enthusiasms, and echoes of old laughter. But it's a feeble search, really. I see things wanting her to see them. I visit places wanting her to be with me. I think thoughts wanting her to share them, crying out for her praise. All that I do from the drinks I drink to the gardens I grow, from the colours I adore to the moods I make – all, everything is the pale reflection of her vivid personality.

We never recover, do we? With her the laughter turned into

cries of pain; without her the laughter is gone. We never really recover.

[*When* BEATRICE *turns to him she is a changed woman. The venom of her words is matched by the hardness in her eyes.*]

BEATRICE: You dare tell me all this?

ADAM: Dare? I confide in you. Why 'dare'?

BEATRICE: Not one thought should you be thinking that is not directed at me.

ADAM: Beatrice!

BEATRICE: At me! Not one thought.

ADAM: But I'm trusting you. With confidences, I'm trusting you.

BEATRICE: And I trusted you. With my love.

ADAM: You've not understood.

BEATRICE: You, my 'golden eagle'.

ADAM: I've just exposed myself.

BEATRICE: My husband always said I expected too much from people.

ADAM: You can't have been listening.

BEATRICE: To make me witness to such insensitivity.

ADAM: Insensitivity?

BEATRICE: Such crudeness.

ADAM: Did you want passionate lies?

BEATRICE: Passionate lies? Is that what our time has been? Your singing, your poetry recitals, your declarations from the clouds? Passionate lies?

ADAM: I know these battlegrounds, Beatrice, don't let's pursue them.

BEATRICE: Why not? Afraid of what might be said? My brave hero? My 'golden eagle'?

ADAM: Let's be wise, recognize the warning. We're tired, don't let's pursue familiar battlegrounds.

[ADAM *retreats from her by taking a drawing pad in which he continues a drawing through the window.*]

BEATRICE: Familiar for us both.

ADAM: For us both then. And so you should understand. Be generous and understand. I listened to your laments, now be generous, listen to my fears. Look at you, you're shaking with rage, you're not even listening.

BEATRICE: I hear every word.

ADAM: You hear what you want to hear, you understand what you need to understand.

BEATRICE [*mocking*]: You see things wanting her to see them, you think thoughts wanting her to share them – face me!

ADAM: You're right.

BEATRICE: Face me!

ADAM: I've made a mistake.

BEATRICE: Face me!

ADAM: I was insensitive. I'm sorry. Now let this day pass.

BEATRICE: Oh no! Not like that you don't dismiss me. I've a right to be answered.

ADAM: Rights? Rights? We now demand rights.

BEATRICE [*suddenly understanding*]: You're afraid.

ADAM: A growing tree blots out the sun.

BEATRICE: I raised my arms to the sun and you were afraid.

ADAM: Yes, afraid. And look how you know it.

BEATRICE: I grow and you become terrified.

ADAM: Yes, yes, terrified; and stop pretending all that innocence.

BEATRICE: You poor thing you.

ADAM: Every time a woman raises her arms to the sun for the man she wants a great battle-cry goes up and the war is declared again.

BEATRICE: You poor, pathetic thing, you.

ADAM: And I try to believe it can't be true, not all the time, but there it is – declared again.

BEATRICE: There's neither fight nor love in you.

[*Pause.*]

ADAM: No love in me? You think that? I'll not fight you, Beatrice. I'm neither pathetic nor afraid, just weary.

[*Long pause.*]

BEATRICE: Why do you draw? A professor of words why do you dabble in shapes? You're not very good at it.

ADAM: Oh your sneering is too accomplished for me.

BEATRICE: I'm not sneering, you just can't draw. Why this need for hobbies? Don't your students adore you enough? The great authority on Romantic poets? Why this need for weekend pastimes?

ADAM: I'm weary, Beatrice, weary and sick.

BEATRICE: Sick? Psychosomatic. You look perfectly healthy to me. Trying to avoid me by retreating into illness?

ADAM: How could I, how could I have made the same mistake again?

BEATRICE: Poor Adam.

ADAM: You don't say 'poor Beatrice'?

BEATRICE: Why should I?

ADAM: No indeed, why should you.

[*They are not facing each other.*
There is a long silence.]

BEATRICE: Adam? I'm cold.

ADAM: The leaves are falling, there's a heavy wind.

BEATRICE: I need something to keep me warm. [*Silence.*] No suggestions these days? Your lady's cold. [*Silence.*] And your silence is even colder. Adam, your poor lady is cold.

[*From a drawer he takes out two pullovers. One is brown, the other is rust.*
The brown one he puts on himself, the other he pulls down over
BEATRICE.
They are now dressed in autumnal colours, green, golden, brown and rust.]

BEATRICE: Why don't *you* warm me?

[*He needs to, fears to, but finally takes her in his arms.*
He kisses her, a long, long kiss.
The light changes.
The days pass, the weeks, even.]

[*Suddenly* ADAM *falls limp in her arms.*]

BEATRICE: Adam! Oh, it's games now is it? Adam!

Really, it's very boyish and charming but I'm a mature woman, games irritate me. [*She waits.*] Adam, don't weary me, please. [*She lowers him to the divan and moves away to attend to the room.*] Adam, I know you want to cheer me up but I'm afraid that some of the games you play are not right for the age we have. Adam! Adam! [*She moves to him and turns him over.*] My God, how white your face has turned. ADAM! [*She places her hand on his forehead.*] But there was no sign. What've you caught you foolish boy? There was no sign. Such a fever – foolish boy, such a fever.

[*She lays a blanket over him and then pulls a small table and armchair to the bedside. From a sideboard she withdraws a bottle of brandy and a glass which she places to* ADAM's *lips.*
When he has drunk some she kisses him.
During her next words the light again changes as she spends the next weeks looking after him.]

Now you are so precious, so precious to me. I would die tending to you.

[ADAM *moves and murmurs.*]

I'm here, my lovely one, right here. No need to cry out. Hush. Lie still, I'm here, feel me. [*She places a blanket round her shoulders and sits by his side to await his recovery.*] How I wish I could sing now. You're right, it *is* a kind of crippling when your voice can't make music. You know, I'm not really as treacherous as I sound, or cold or humourless. Sometimes a fever gets in me too and I don't know what I say. But I'm always honest, at least to myself, and good and really – very wise.

But I'm damaged, I blush for the creases in my skin, I'm ashamed of my worn limbs, second-hand. Third-hand to be precise; third-hand bruised and damaged – like a clock striking midnight when the hour is only six, and it wheezes and whirrs.

But if we'd met each other before we'd met anyone else then the right hour would have sung clear and ringing at the right time, every time. If, if, if . . . Oh, Adam. And what wouldn't we have done together then? Raised storms among the dead – that's what we'd have done then. Do you know what my husband once said to me? 'You're like a queen,' he said, 'without her country. I hate queens,' he said, 'without their countries.'

And he was right. A queen without a country, or a king. No home and no man to pay me homage. All my life I've looked for peace and majesty, for a man who was unafraid and generous; generous and not petty. I can't bear little men: mean, apologetic, timid men, men who mock themselves and sneer at others, who delight in downfall and dare nothing. Peace, majesty and great courage – how I've longed for these things.

He once abandoned me in a fog, that man, that man I called 'God'; in a long, London fog, left me, to walk home alone.

Peace, majesty and great courage.

And once I ran through a storm and stood on a station platform, soaking and full of tears, pleading with him to take me, take me, take me with him. And he wanted to take me, I know it, because we loved walking through streets in strange towns discovering new shapes to the houses and breathing new airs, but he refused to show this need.

Peace, majesty and great courage – never. I've found none of these things. Such bitter disappointment. Bitter. Bitter, bitter, bitter. And out of such bitterness cruelty grows. You can't understand the cruelty that grows. And I meant none of it, not one cruel word of it. And he knew and I knew and we both knew that we knew, yet the cruelty went on.

But laments for what's done and past are not a way to cure an invalid are they? I should be making plans for tomorrow shouldn't I? For when you get up, and the day after, and the month after and all those long years we'll have together. What shall we do in those years, Adam? Eh? All those great long years ahead? Shall we set to right 'The silly world's intolerable pains'? I have plans, of children and travel and daring all those things you didn't dare before. We'll plot and build each moment like two brilliant lovers. And peace, above all – peace, and trust and majesty and all that great courage.

Get well my darling boy and you'll see. My voice may not sing but my love does. Get well.

[ADAM *sits up.*]

ADAM: How long has it been?

BEATRICE: The weeks have passed.

ADAM: And have you stayed with me that long?

BEATRICE: Hush.

ADAM: Weeks? And you've stayed with me all that time?

BEATRICE: Yes. But don't imagine it was an effort because it wasn't. It sounds more heroic than it was, I suffer from insomnia, it came easily.

ADAM: What a strange fever it was. I've never been so ill before.

BEATRICE: Fatigue, tension, quite common really.

ADAM: Don't take the drama out of it. I feel weak and sad and I'm enjoying it. If only you were as tender and generous as this always.

BEATRICE: Aren't I?

No, I'm not. But consider, how else do we know to sneer at others if not because we've sneered at ourselves so well?

ADAM [*he moves to look at his drawing pad*]: You're right of course. I dabble. I should be content with words, even though they're other people's words.

BEATRICE: I dabble also. That's how I recognize the dabbler, the dilettante.

You don't contradict me? That's not very gallant.

ADAM: You know what *I* think. You have an original mind. You don't need me for flattery.

BEATRICE: How wrong you are. To believe in the nonsense of honesty, how wrong you are. I need to hear you say I have an original mind and more, and more, to compensate for my deficiencies, my failings.

ADAM: Was I sick? My stomach feels so empty, I feel so thin. And you stayed through the smell and ugliness of all that? [*Rises from sick bed, blanket over his shoulders, looks out of window.*] The days get shorter. You can smell the days getting shorter. We've known each other a long time now haven't we?

[*Both in their separate places let the blankets drop from their shoulders. The days pass, the weeks, even.*]

[*The preparation for the strudel. Complete change to exuberant mood.*]

ADAM: It's a long time since I've made one. Two things my grandmother bequeathed me in her will, a bag full of mint farthings and the recipe for Hungarian apple strudel. [*He is looking for white aprons.*] Here, *you'll* also need to wear one. The dust flies, I warn you. [*He wrings his hands, like a pianist before the concert, exaggerating the movements.*] You know, my son used to say that the colour of the wind was black.

BEATRICE: That's depressing.

ADAM: No, it's positive. Black! He was certain of it, couldn't be any other colour. Black! And he used to smile as though I must be teasing to ask a question with such an obvious answer.

BEATRICE: What colour do you think it is?

ADAM: Grey. The wind is grey.

And now, the miracle.

BEATRICE [*sceptically*]: The miracle! I've been waiting so long for this miracle.

ADAM: It's magical, I promise you. Everything prepared?

BEATRICE: As you asked for. Sliced apples, cleaned nuts.

ADAM: The rest?

BEATRICE: Raisins, caster sugar, cinnamon and olive oil.

[BEATRICE *brings these items out on to the sideboard.*

ADAM *is about to make apple strudel;** the process is a very dramatic one.*

---

* Culinary notes are at the end of the play.

The paste has been 'resting' for twenty minutes. He is about to collect it from the kitchen. But first he throws a table-cloth over the table. The magician prepares!

Now he retrieves the paste from the kitchen; it is lying on a plate, covered by a floured cloth. The paste sits like a round loaf. He picks it from the plate, gingerly since it flops about, though it should come away clean if the plate has been well floured, and he is about to lay it on the centre of the table.]

ADAM: The flour!

In the kitchen, quick, I took it there to dust this plate. For God's sake, the paste is drooping, quick.

[BEATRICE *hastens to find the flour and returns to dust, sprinkle, strew the table-cloth with it.*

ADAM *lays his paste in the centre of the cloth, reaches for a rolling pin, dusts that with flour, and rolls it out to the first oval stage.]*

ADAM: Pretty?

[BEATRICE *shrugs her shoulders.]*

You're a hard woman, Beatrice.

BEATRICE: Hard? How short-sighted you are. I'm soft, like this dough, only a bit tastier.

ADAM: You've made a joke. You didn't mean to but you made a joke. It's the first time.

BEATRICE: Your paste, attend to your paste.

ADAM: Hard. Not a bit of praise. Mean.

BEATRICE: When you've earned your praise I'll give it, lavishly. Your paste.

ADAM: Oil, hot oil, in the kitchen.

[*He holds out his hand like a doctor calling for the scalpel, never taking his eyes off the paste.*

A sceptical BEATRICE *moves slowly off.]*

Move, woman. Quick.

[ADAM *is delighted and walks round and round his paste.]*

BEATRICE: 'Quick!' he cries.

[*But she does move faster and brings* ADAM *his oil. He pours a thimbleful over the paste and then spreads it over the surface with his palm.]*

ADAM: Ouch! it's hot. Now [*to himself*] make sure it covers the surface, help it stretch, gently, and – wait.

Now, you just sit there, and – watch.

[*He looks triumphantly at* BEATRICE *who again shrugs her shoulders.*]
Hard, so hard.

BEATRICE: You find delight in such small things.

ADAM: Small things? Small things? You've seen nothing, nothing yet.
The miracle begins now. [*And sure enough, the miracle does begin
now, for* ADAM *begins to stretch his paste and does so to the accompani-
ment of much gentle clowning; gentle, gentle, not frantic, clowning.*]
Pull, my beauty, pull, pull. Stay moist, don't harden yet, stay
moist.

[BEATRICE *impatiently rises and turns her attention to the room.*]
Why do you keep emptying ashtrays and tidying up?
Keep still and watch me.

BEATRICE: Dirt offends me.

ADAM: You can't cope with disorder, can you?

BEATRICE: Yes, I can cope with disorder, only dirt and ugly things I
can't bear.

ADAM: You're so fussy.

BEATRICE: No. Fussiness belongs to pedants. I'm not a pedant, just
right!

[*He brings her back to the chair to ensure she is watching before
resuming his work.*]

ADAM: A hole! Damn, a hole! Lack of practice. Still, not a big one.
Must keep my eye on that, have to patch it if it grows.

BEATRICE: I'm sure the clowning and gestures are not essential.

ADAM: Cruel. You're cruel and hard. Here, drink some milk, soften
yourself.

BEATRICE: I can't bear milk. It's for women who throw javelins. I
prefer lemons.

ADAM: Sour. Sour and hard. Your eyes should be growing wider and
wider. You should be astonished at my skill.

BEATRICE: I confess – it's fascinating.

ADAM: How begrudgingly you say it. Damn, another hole. Small, it's
small though. Wha hoo! Wha hoo! [ADAM *has reached the stage
where he can flap the pastry, like a sheet on a bed, to straighten it
out.*] Isn't that a marvellous sight?

BEATRICE: Very clever, yes.

ADAM: Why, you're irritated.

BEATRICE: Am I?

ADAM: Why are you irritated?

BEATRICE: Look, another hole, attend to your holes.

ADAM: Why are you so irritated?

BEATRICE: I'm sorry. I can't share your miracle.

ADAM: Of course you can. Learn, you can learn can't you? Tomorrow you'll make one. You're jealous aren't you?

BEATRICE: Jealous!

ADAM: Ha ha! She's jealous. Pull, my beauty, pull, pull. Did I ever tell you about my student days? About the time I nearly set fire to the kitchen I worked in? I dipped a panier of wet chips into boiling hot fat. Don't laugh. I thought the wet chips would cool the fat down; no one ever told me that when you put water to hot fat it ignites.

BEATRICE: What happened?

ADAM: It ignited! I just stood there, watching the flames, mesmerized. And the chefs and maintenance men ran backwards and forwards screaming and trying to smother the flames with some sticky stuff and I just stood there, watching. Of course I was paralysed with surprise so I stood still, and everyone thought I was being calm. I ended the hero.

There, it's done. And only a few holes. Now apples. [*He strews apples along the edge of the table.*] Cinnamon. [*He dusts with cinnamon.*] Nuts. [*He strews the nuts.*] Raisins. [*He scatters the raisins.*] Sugar. [*He attends to the sugar.*] More cinnamon. [ADAM *sprinkles another coat of cinnamon.*] Clean up. [*And takes a knife and cuts away the thick edges of paste hanging all around the table.*] Now we roll. [ADAM *clutches each end of the table-cloth under the hanging paste and gently rolls and encloses the contents of the strudel into a long pipe. When it's done he hastily drips more olive oil over the surface of the long strudel, sprinkles more sugar into the oil, cuts it into three lengths, lays the three lengths on to an oven tray and, swiftly, pushes all into the oven snapping the door shut in triumph.*] Now, tell me, why are you so irritated?

BEATRICE: You were so absorbed.

ADAM: But I did it for you. For you to watch, for you to learn, for you to eat.

BEATRICE: That's how it started, perhaps. But half-way through I –

ADAM: What? Half-way through you –

BEATRICE: I'm so stupid and ashamed.

ADAM: You –?

BEATRICE: I became afraid.

ADAM: Afraid?

BEATRICE: Oh don't go on. If you can't understand don't go on.

ADAM: You can't dismiss me like that – I want to understand.

BEATRICE: You just want me to say it don't you?

ADAM: Yes.

BEATRICE: It's your laughter. I can't bear your laughter, it's unnatural. It casts everybody out.

ADAM: Everybody?

BEATRICE: Well me, then.

ADAM: You resent my laughter?

BEATRICE: Every second. Every touch, every thought, every feeling, every second you should give to me.

ADAM: And then there would come a moment when every touch would be flinched from, every thought sneered at and every feeling abused.

BEATRICE: And that's the moment you're afraid of?

ADAM: Yes.

BEATRICE: You think me capable of abuse?

ADAM: All women.

BEATRICE: But me? Me? Capable of abuse?

ADAM: All women.

BEATRICE: I see.

[*The tidying is done.*

They move apart.

The days are passing, the weeks, even.]

AUTUMN

The walls and the furniture move. They stand, each alone, looking at the sky; a wind blows.

The light changes from dusk to night. It is a brilliantly clear, brisk night, full of stars.

BEATRICE: What are you thinking?

ADAM: If I said my mind's a blank, would you believe me?

BEATRICE: If you say so.

[*Pause.*]

Is it?

[*Pause.*]

Do those stars only inspire blankness?

[*Pause.*]

Why didn't you love your wife?

ADAM: Why didn't *you* love your husband?

BEATRICE: Why? There are no reasons. One day you just look at somebody and realize you don't love them. No hate, no anger —

ADAM: Just guilt for being unable to feel what's expected and needed from you. You know, I can't think of anything I've done that I haven't felt guilty for.

The first girl I ever loved was when I was twelve years old. She had a pink face and a cheeky smile and she thought she was ugly. I couldn't persuade her that she wasn't. She pouted her lips and protected herself behind large, wise eyes as if she knew before love came that love was an impossible dream. For four years I wooed her until, at last, a moment came when she finally trusted herself in my arms; and in that moment, that very same moment, I betrayed her.

It happened at a camp in a valley, near one of the largest forests I'd ever seen. We went each summer, for four years, just a group of us.

And on the last summer there came a girl who took one look at me and decided — what were her own words now? She told me afterwards — she had decided, from the start, to 'net me'. Net me! What a woman in the making she was. Tongue like a whip. Will, like a great boulder; and intelligence, sharp, like a frightened hawk. And I was to carry her scars for ever. Because while I wooed my childhood sweetheart this miniature adult weaved her own and subtle net with a terrible, terrible precision. And on the last night she, my wide-eyed sweetheart, and I, at last, after four years, managed, somehow, to find that sort of exhaustion which earned us the trust of each other's arms. I'd won. There we lay, among friends and the smell of wet canvas — she wasn't really in my arms but on them, and I think I kissed her cheek, once, or perhaps twice, nothing more, and then she fell asleep. And as she was lying on my arm, another hand reached out for me, and — I took it.

I lie here, under these stars, and I think about camp and remember that camp and I know, as sure as I know that there's a cloud on that moon, that for that one terrible act of betrayal I have paid and wrecked my once and only life with every act and decision I've ever made. That's what I'm thinking.

Do you know, a friend and I once ran all the way across three fields and up a hill to see a sun set? Without stopping, all the way, imagine that – I ran, like a lunatic, to catch a sun setting on some Cotswold hill.

How difficult it is to believe we were ever once happy.

[*Long pause. Tries to lighten the mood.*]

Allow me to show you a photograph of one of my children. Do you know I've never shown a photograph of my children to anyone before? Always considered people who did that were boorish. Won't embarrass you, will it? Look at that grin. Look at the way his arms fold. Defiant! That's him. Stubborn and defiant, in charge!

[ADAM *strikes the pose of the child in the photograph.*]

BEATRICE: Yes, he looks like you. What is it pasted to? A Christmas card? Of your son?

ADAM: It's a Christmas card of a child.

BEATRICE: He actually sent a Christmas card with a photograph of his son on it. What bad taste. I blush for you.

ADAM: I sent it because it's a good photograph of a child, not because it's my son.

BEATRICE: Like a politician endearing himself to the public. You have children like possessions don't you? Did you show it to your mistress? Every time you made love? Did you? Take it out and sigh over it, to show how guilty you felt? Did you talk about your wife in bed? Say how good she really was? Did you? Did you tell your other mistress the story of the girl at camp? The one with the large wise eyes? Did you? Did you? DID YOU?

ADAM: You're possessed aren't you? Something moves in you that you can't control doesn't it? Can't you hear yourself? Don't you ever feel ashamed? The same, always the same sneers, always the same mockeries and sneers. All my life I've looked for a woman who had that touch of magic. Passion without deceit, wisdom without cruelty, pity without abuse.

BEATRICE: A Christmas card of your son!

ADAM: You've not even heard. Not one word have you heard. You can neither hear nor understand that you're not hearing.

BEATRICE: I think I see you now. Go home to your wife. She'll forgive you. There's nothing more you can do here.

ADAM: *You*'ve never dared to have a child, have you?

BEATRICE: No man with any sensitivity would have said that.

ADAM: You make up the rules as you go along.

BEATRICE: My 'golden eagle'. His son on a Christmas card.

ADAM: It was not love you needed was it? Was it? I don't think you're capable of love are you? Eh? Capable of it? Are you capable of real love?

BEATRICE: Yes.

ADAM: Really capable?

BEATRICE: Yes, yes.

ADAM: Are you?

BEATRICE: Yes, yes. Love. Real love. I – CAN – LOVE.

ADAM: How loudly you need to say it.

BEATRICE: I – can – love. I – have – loved. Always. And look what comes back – the pathetic smell of guilt. I – can – love.

ADAM: The sounds you make, I know you make the sounds, the sounds and the gestures of love. But feelings? Nothing.

BEATRICE: My dear, you're not the best person to talk about feelings are you? Ah those nights at camp with – what was it? – the smell of wet canvas?

ADAM: Nothing, nothing can be trusted with you.

BEATRICE: Don't imagine you confided things to me that I couldn't already see.

ADAM: I gave you what was precious to me. What you needed I gave you and it was precious to me.

BEATRICE: You? You were never big enough to give me what I needed. But I'll survive.

ADAM: Won't you just.

BEATRICE: I've more guts and passion than the three of you together. I'll survive.

ADAM: Won't you, won't you, just!

BEATRICE: I warned you. I asked you to come away from this place.

ADAM: That's the reason is it?

BEATRICE: Now go home.

ADAM: Because I didn't fly off with you?

BEATRICE: You couldn't keep one mistress, give this one up. Go home.

ADAM: Because you couldn't wait to bring back the spoils?

BEATRICE [mocking]: You see things wanting her to see them, you think thoughts wanting her to share them – go home.

ADAM: You failed two men and now you need to show that it wasn't your fault.

BEATRICE: Who can't be trusted with confessions, who?

ADAM: Oh, you're righteous about betrayal now are you?

BEATRICE: You dare throw back at me what I confided in you?

ADAM: You drag dirt from me.

BEATRICE: Go home to your comforts.

ADAM: You oppress me.

BEATRICE: To your wife, go home.

ADAM: You dry up the air around me.

BEATRICE: To your grinning brats – go, go.

[ADAM *slaps her face.*]

You dare lift your hands to me? You dare?

[*She raises her hands to attack him but he holds her wrists.*]

ADAM: Nothing touches you. You devour, devour, devour, DEVOUR!

BEATRICE: I despise you. Go home.

[*He releases her.*
The walls return, the furniture also.
The days pass, the weeks, even.]

[BEATRICE *creeps to a corner of the room, retreating once more into misery and tears.*]

BEATRICE: I saw God in you.

ADAM: You saw in me what you needed to see in me.

[*She is crying.*]

You cry for yourself.

BEATRICE: I cry for you.

ADAM: For your own misery.

BEATRICE: For you, for you. I cry for you.

ADAM: I believe neither you nor your tears.

BEATRICE: Couldn't you see I whipped you from fear?

ADAM: Couldn't you see I retreated from fear?

BEATRICE: I don't know what I say.

ADAM: You know everything you say, only too well, you know everything.

BEATRICE: I'm so vulnerable and frightened.

ADAM: Frightened? You?

BEATRICE: Help me.

ADAM: I cannot.

BEATRICE: I give you my hand. Help me.

ADAM: I cannot.

BEATRICE: Let's make up. Like children. Let's do something silly. Climb a tree with me. Look at the moon with me. Like children, let's make up.

ADAM: If only I could. How well you know how to tempt me, don't you? Like children, make up, if only I could.

BEATRICE: Like children, Adam, a pact, like children.

ADAM: And then would come another moment and it would be as though no pact had ever existed and you would spit and spit and spit again, and then you would ask to be comforted and then again you'd spit and I'd be tossed from the right hand of your passion to the left hand of your venom and I cannot, I cannot, I cannot.

BEATRICE: Help me.

ADAM: I cannot.

[BEATRICE *now utters a terrifying moan that begins like a wail of despair but rises to a cry of anger – as though half way through her wail she realises that it will have no effect and her plea will be unanswered. The cry ends abruptly. Both realize that the year has ended.*

BEATRICE *moves to the chest of drawers and meticulously brings out the clothes to fold them ready for packing. Her calm is chilling.*]

BEATRICE: You know, there was nothing between us really, was there?

ADAM: Wasn't there?

BEATRICE: We weren't even really friends, were we?

ADAM: No?

BEATRICE: My husband always used to say to me I expected too much from people.

ADAM: What more?

BEATRICE: What more is there to say? Nothing happened. It was all play-acting. A girlish dream. I'm surprised at myself that I can still have girlish dreams. Nothing, nothing at all, nothing happened.

ADAM: No of course not, it was foolishness wasn't it? It's always foolish to try and know more than one person. To know more than one person is to betray them.

BEATRICE: On the contrary, to know only one person is to betray the world.

ADAM: Ah yes, the world.

BEATRICE: You can never be an island you know.

ADAM: Oh? Do you think that when the millennium comes there won't be lovers who grow weary of their sad girls, or that wives won't weep over empty beds? Even when Jerusalem is built friends will grow apart and mothers will mourn their sons growing old.

Do you want me to feel for starving children? I feel for them. Do you want me to protest at wars that go on in the mountains? I protest. But the heart has its private aches. Not all the good great causes in this world can stop me crying for a passing love.

[*Long pause. They need to comfort, forgive one another, somehow.*]

Beatrice, what do you remember most about him?

BEATRICE: What do I remember?

A long drive into the autumn countryside I remember. The astonishment we shared that trees and fields could burn with such colours. The tremendous blaze of dying hedges, the smouldering leaves, the discovery of these things.

I remember the plots against indifference, the ease with which we picked up each other's thoughts in our 'battles with the world', the language we gave each other, my gratitude for his presence, my helplessness. I remember that we weren't afraid to laugh hysterically or to play with children or to grow old. I remember we were not afraid.

And I remember that when my father died in a far-off country I didn't go to his side because I wanted to stay with *him*. And my father died alone – I was his favourite child. These things I remember. And you? Tell me what you remember about her.

ADAM: Moments of music and silence and adoration I remember. I remember the scrupulous care she gave to everything she did for me, binding a present, cooking a meal. The attention of her eyes. I remember my cruelty and I remember her cruelty.

I remember that we weren't afraid to dance when we couldn't, to say we didn't know things we should have known or admit each wrong we'd committed against the other.

I remember my father dying and my holding his head in my hands and crying, 'Keep breathing, come on, don't give up, Joe, don't stop, Joe.' And my mother, through her tears, saying, 'You think he'll listen to you?' and smiling, and both of us sobbing and smiling.

[*They exchange smiles.*]

These things I remember. Because moments like these remind me that time passes and time passing reminds me of sadness and waste and neglect and suffering. And I know in my heart that all those lovely moments of youth will never return, and so it's easier for me to forgive and hope to be forgiven. These things, Beatrice.

BEATRICE: I think I have an illness coming on. I'm feeling cold.

ADAM: Cold? Yes, it is cold isn't it? Shall we try and warm ourselves? Those dead leaves you swept up this morning – I'll start a fire with those. [*He moves quickly to the grate where the leaves are piled.*]

BEATRICE: I don't know why I should be so cold.

ADAM: We'll soon be warm. [*He tries to light the leaves. They only smoulder.*] They're damp.

BEATRICE: Autumn leaves. Dead. What did you expect?

[*He blows hard to bring them to flame.*]

ADAM: Burn, damn you, burn!

They won't light.

[ADAM *watches the feeble smoke.* BEATRICE *folds and folds and meticulously folds* –]

EPILOGUE

The Four Seasons sets out to explore only the essentials of a relationship with deliberately little recourse to explanation or background; but the dialogue is heightened, the form highly stylized and the metaphor of the play simple; there lay the dangers both for understanding and performing the work. The heightened dialogue invites the 'poetic' rendering; the high stylization invites portentous direction; and the simplicity of the metaphor – equating stages of love with the passing of the seasons – tempts one to suspect there must be 'more to it than that'. There is not. Adam does not represent 'man' nor Beatrice 'woman', nor is the deserted house a womb. It is a play neither of allegory nor symbols; the scenes and sequences of events are nothing more than they seem.

Yet conscious that a wilful withholding of certain information might cause an audience to pursue irrelevant questions, it seemed right to present that kind of information which would ensure concentration on the relationship alone. A major problem then: what kind of information? That which seemed inevitable. For instance, neither Adam nor Beatrice mentions to whom the house belongs. Adam could have said it belonged to his father but such information is timid; it would have jarred and made no difference to their subsequent relationship.* Beatrice spends the entire season of winter in silence and immobility; she could have pottered around, attempted the mechanical motions of survival but – such action is feeble; the form would have been cluttered.

In writing the play I confronted one other major problem: how to avoid the trap of creating a pseudo-poetic dialogue; and one major consideration: can one recreate a love relationship and ignore any recognizable social context?

The first: the words and rhythms of everyday speech are rich and

---

* I changed my mind in 1981. It seemed to be just the kind of information the withholding of which would 'cause an audience to pursue irrelevant information'. I made the house belong to Adam's uncle to whom I also gave a fleeting personality which I hoped would immediately set the play in a real rather than abstract world.

contain their own poetry, but after a time they cease to be adequate. In six plays (*Their Very Own and Golden City* was written before *The Four Seasons*) I had wrung from such speech rhythms all that I was able, at least for the moment, and wanted to create a heightened and lyrical language. Of course pretentiousness had to be avoided, but the problem of using current English dialogue lay in its impoverishment; it is a real and disturbing problem.

Let me give an example. In the rehearsal script of the play and throughout the production Adam told Beatrice that she had 'autumn soft skin'. For me this conjured up the image of walks through the wind and soft rich colours of autumn landscapes – until someone insisted the image belonged more to a television advert for Camay soap. I resisted the suggestion at first but finally acknowledged it and deleted the words. Then it occurred to me how much of our language had been abused by such misuse. The suggestion that a box of chocolates brings 'eternal happiness', that 'love blossoms' with the right toothpaste, that 'peace' comes with a cigarette, that 'manhood dawns' with a certain kind of beer. And more: not only have words been denied us by misuse, not only have I spent six plays on everyday rhythms but, since *Look Back in Anger*, there have been so many plays exploiting the vitality of current idioms, to say nothing of those endless tales of everyday life turned out by television. This is not to denigrate ordinary speech or attack the plays which followed *Look Back* and *Root*, I'm simply stating a fact about the nature of artistic development over which the artist has little control, namely this: certain devices as well as certain fields of human behaviour offer only a limited fund of inspiration for the artist or, nearer the truth, they offer an endless fund for only a limited time.

The second: there is an argument which says that individual or private pain can have no relevance in a society where man's real tragedies are bound inextricably with his social environment; a story unrelated to and ignoring social and political events is a story that has no truth or validity. To which I make this reply: If compassion and teaching the possibility of change are two of the many effects of art, a third is this: to remind and reassure people that they are not alone not only in their attempts to make a better world but in their private pains and confusions also. The terrible sneers and ridicule that private pain in art has attracted from socialists has helped create the intimidating image of the socialist as cold-hearted and relentlessly chastising, and is perhaps why so many people on the left manifest the same puritanical attitudes towards art and the artist which are shared by a perplexed, narrow-minded bourgeoisie. There is no abandoning in this play of concern for socialist principles nor a turning away from a preoccupation with real human problems; on the contrary, the play, far from being a retreat from values contained in my early writing, is a logical extension of them in that a connection exists between, for instance, Sara Kahn's cry 'love comes first, you can't have brotherhood without love' and Beatrice's lament that 'without love I have neither appetite nor desire, I'm capable of nothing'.

Deny plays such as this as a part of socialist literature and you alienate all men and women who need to know and be comforted by the knowledge that they are not alone in their private pain. You can urge mankind to no action by intimidating it with your eternal condemnation of its frailties. *The Four Seasons* was written because I believe the absence of love diminishes and distorts all action.

A.W.

NOTES

The Apple Strudel
The process of making apple strudel is a very dramatic one and involves patience and experience. But actors learn to fence – why not to cook? The art lies in the pulling and stretching of the paste over a cloth covering the entire table until the paste is paper thin and hanging over the edges. Apples, raisins, nuts, cinnamon, and sugar are now strewn along the length of the paste, which is rolled into a long pipe of strudel. This is done by pulling the cloth from under the paste which you then flick forward.

The problem is not to make holes in the pulling. Holes invariably appear and if they are small can be ignored; if they are large then they need to be patched up by tearing a piece off the edge.

The movement required is a beautiful one where the cook moves round and round the table pulling here, pulling there, not too much at a time, not too quickly, and most of the time using the back of his hand under the paste, drawing his hand towards him, rather than the fingers which would make holes. After a while the confident cook can flap the paste in order to straighten it out. To watch this being done is really exciting and the best chefs clown while they do it.

When the paste has been stretched till the edges are hanging over four sides of the table the chef must move swiftly, or the paste, being so thin, will dry up. Obviously the thinner the paste becomes the more tense everyone is.

The paste is made of $1\frac{1}{2}$ lb. flour, $\frac{3}{4}$ pt. water, a pinch of salt, one egg and 2 teaspoonfuls of olive oil. It must be pummelled for a long time – in an automatic beater – until the mixture is smooth and pliable, just short of being tacky. The longer it is beaten the easier it is to stretch. It is left to rest for about twenty minutes, and then it is rolled out with a rolling pin into an oval shape about 18 ins. by 9 ins., a quarter of an inch thick. Next a film of hot olive oil is rubbed gently over the entire surface and left to sink in for thirty seconds; then the pulling begins.

Little of this preparation is done in the play. The paste and ingredients are ready in time for the scene. Only the pulling and filling are acted.

Advice should be sought from a high-class pastrycook.

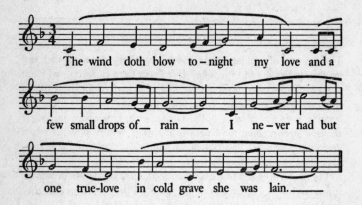

The wind doth blow to-night my love and a few small drops of rain I ne-ver had but one true-love in cold grave she was lain.

Their Very Own and Golden City

A PLAY IN TWO ACTS
AND MANY SCENES

TO MY DEAR FRIEND TOM MASCHLER

PREFACE
TO REVISED EDITION

To Henryk Bering Liisberg,* the director of the municipal theatre of the Danish city of Aarhus, and to his company of actors and technicians I owe an enormous debt of gratitude for giving me the facilities to direct this difficult play almost entirely as I wanted. No expense was spared.

In doing so I fell in love with the work again. Of course it's too ambitious, the theme belongs to the cinema, it stretches across more time and action than the theatre should properly handle. Yet I promise the reader it is worth struggling to read through the involved stage directions, for lumber though it does yet it lumbers with a daring we all found exhilarating.

After the London productions in which the director made the mistaken and crippling decision (with which I foolishly agreed) to have one set of actors play both the old and young protagonists, I thought the play was irretrievably flawed. But with the help of the Danish actors and through the brilliant set of Hayden Griffen I came to understand the play better and to discover that, though it attempts too much, it is not *irretrievably* flawed. It *does* work.

I owe my discovery of this to the faith of

HENRYK BERING LIISBERG

to whom this new edition is dedicated.

London, 12 December 1980

*Now Director General of the Royal Theatre, Copenhagen.

The world premiere of *Their Very Own and Golden City* was at the Belgian National Theatre in 1965. The first London presentation of the play opened on 19 May 1966 and was directed at the Royal Court Theatre by William Gaskill, sets by Christopher Morley, with the following cast:

ANDREW COBHAM	Ian McKellen
JESSIE SUTHERLAND	Gillian Martell
JOHN CASPER	George Howe
JAKE LATHAM	Sebastian Shaw
SMITHY	Bernard Gallagher
KATE RAMSAY	Ann Firbank
PRIEST	Roger Booth
STONEY JACKSON	William Stewart
PAUL DOBSON	John Shepherd
CHAIRMAN OF LOCAL TOWN PLANNING COMMITTEE	Richard Butler
REGINALD MAITLAND	Sebastian Shaw
TED WORTHINGTON	Bernard Gallagher
BILL MATHESON	Richard Butler
BRIAN CAMBRIDGE	Joseph Greig
TOASTMASTER	Roger Booth
MAISY	Jannette Legge
GUESTS, ETC.	David Leland
	Jaqueline Harrison
	Janet Chappell
	Jannette Legge
	Kenneth Cranham

... and accordingly the Trade Unionists and their leaders who were once the butt of the most virulent abuse from the whole of the Upper and Middle classes are now praised and petted by them because they do tacitly or openly acknowledge the necessity for the master's existence; it is felt that they are no longer the enemy; the class struggle in England is entering into a new phase, which may even make the once dreaded Trade Unions allies of capital, since they in their turn form a kind of privileged group among the workmen; in fact they now no longer represent the whole class of workers as working *men* but rather as charged with the office of keeping the human part of the capitalists' machinery in good working order and freeing it from any grit of discontent ...

Now that's the blind alley which the Trade Unions have now got into; I say again if they are determined to have masters to manage their affairs, they must expect in turn to pay for that luxury ... remembering that the price they pay for their so-called captains of industry is no mere money payment – no mere tribute which once paid leaves them free to do as they please, but an authoritative ordering of the whole tenor of their lives, what they shall eat, drink, wear, what houses they shall have, books, or newspapers rather, they shall read, down to the very days on which they shall take their holidays like a drove of cattle driven from the stable to grass.

WILLIAM MORRIS: *from a lecture on 'Socialism' given at the Victoria Hall, Norwich, on 8 March 1886*

LIST OF CHARACTERS

ACT I

ANDREW COBHAM	⎫
JESSIE SUTHERLAND	⎬ *as youngsters*
PAUL DOBSON	
STONEY JACKSON	⎭
ANDREW COBHAM	*an architect*
JESSIE SUTHERLAND	*his wife*
PAUL DOBSON	*a journalist*
STONEY JACKSON	*a minister*
JAKE LATHAM	*an old trade union organizer*
SMITHY	*a local Labour Party chairman*
KATE RAMSAY	*a daughter of local aristocracy*, Jake's *friend*
JOHN CASPER	*an architect*, Andrew's *employer*

ACT II

CHAIRMAN OF LOCAL TOWN PLANNING COMMITTEE
OFFICER OF MINISTRY OF TOWN AND COUNTRY PLANNING
ALFIE HARRINGTON *an industrialist*
REGINALD MAITLAND *Minister of Town and Country Planning*

TED WORTHINGTON	⎫
BILL MATHESON	⎬ *trade union leaders*
BRIAN CAMBRIDGE	⎭

TOASTMASTER

Couples for crowd scenes from whom can be taken three walk-ons.

NOTE

Because of the construction of this play – which is in the form of a 'flash-forward' (as opposed to 'flash-back') – two sets of actors are needed to play ANDREW COBHAM, JESSICA SUTHERLAND, PAUL DOBSON, STONEY JACKSON: one set of young actors to whom we constantly return in the setting of the Cathedral, and another set who will act out the play from being young men and women to old ones. In the London production one set of actors played both parts and this established a particular style to the production.

But in May 1974 the author directed the play in Aarhus, Denmark, where he not only reverted to two sets of actors but also made changes to the play.

This edition incorporates those changes plus directions based on the set designed by HAYDEN GRIFFEN.

The following characters can be played by the same actor:

JAKE LATHAM *and* REGINALD MAITLAND

WORTHINGTON *and* SMITHY

JOHN CASPER *and* ALFIE HARRINGTON

CHAIRMAN *and* MATHESON

THE SET

The basic principle of the set is simple: the 'future' is talked about in the cathedral and therefore must be played-out inside it.

The cathedral setting which is constantly present is composed of a pillar on either side of the stage, a stained-glass window to the rear, a catafalque to the front of the stage (protruding out into the audience?), and two mock-gothic ecclesiastical screens cutting across the centre of the stage which should contain a revolve. Each scene is set up behind the screens which part to allow the setting to be revolved on.

It is in the nature of the play that the sets can begin to move into position while the previous scene is ending, thus ensuring a completely fluid style of production.

SCENES

ACT I:

1 Interior of Durham Cathedral — 1926
2 Casper's architect's office — 1933
3 A riverside — some hours later
4 A public house — some months later
5 Jake's study — some weeks later
6 Andy's bed-sitter — some days later
7 Durham Cathedral — 1926
8 A riverside — 1935
9 Andy's study — 1936
10 Andy's study — some days later
11 A public meeting hall — some months later
12 Durham Cathedral — 1926
13 A Town Hall chamber — 1947

ACT II:

1 The riverside — some days later
2 Andy's study — some weeks later
3 Durham Cathedral — 1926
4 Platform of the T.U.C. — 1948
5 The continuous scene — 1948–85 or thereabouts — moving through these settings:

Part 1 Golden City offices
Part 2 Andy's study
Part 3 Golden City offices
Part 4 Corridor of Ministry of Town and Country Planning
Part 5 Harrington's cocktail party
Part 6 Maitland's cocktail party
Part 7 Golden City offices/Durham Cathedral
Part 8 Office in Trades Union Congress House
Part 9 Golden City offices
Part 10 Andy's study
Part 11 Building site in the Golden City
Part 12 Banquet scene
Part 13 Andy's lounge

Part 14 The card table
Part 15 Durham Cathedral

N.B. If the cathedral scenes in either Act are heavily played this entire play will fail. Innocence, gaiety and a touch of lunacy is their atmosphere.

The author is aware that certain instances in the play do not conform to actual Trade Union or Labour Party procedure, and hopes that the poetic licence he has taken will be understood.

ACT ONE

SCENE ONE

Interior Durham Cathedral.
Music of Thomas Tallis's 40-part motet, Spem in alium.*
Empty stage.
A young man enters, ANDREW COBHAM. *He carries a drawing-board and knapsack. It is the year 1926.*
What he is looking at he is seeing for the first time.
Magic. Discovery.
He could weep for the beauty of the moment.
Instead, exhilarated, he tosses his knapsack into the air.

YOUNG ANDY [*with surprise*]: I – am as big as – it. They built cathedrals for one man – it's just big enough. [*He closes his eyes.*] Show me love ànd I'll hate no one. [JESSICA SUTHERLAND *wanders in.*] Give me wings and I'll build you a city. Teach me to fly and I'll do beautiful deeds. [*He opens his eyes and looks up at the roof.*] Hey God, do you hear that? Beautiful deeds, I said.

YOUNG JESSIE: Andy?

YOUNG ANDY: For one man, Jessie, a cathedral is built for one man.

YOUNG JESSIE: Do you talk to yourself?

YOUNG ANDY: Every man should have a cathedral in his back garden.

YOUNG JESSIE: I've never heard you talk to yourself.

YOUNG ANDY: Look at the way that roof soars.

YOUNG JESSIE: Talk to yourself and you'll go mad.

YOUNG ANDY: Doesn't it make you love yourself?

YOUNG JESSIE: 'Those whom the gods wish to destroy they first turn mad.'

YOUNG ANDY: When a man loves himself he loves the world. Listen.
[*Music swells.*]
I reckon the gods touch composers with a fever every night. I bet Bach got to heaven before Shakespeare. Look.

*(Argo label ZRG 5436)

[*Sunlight strikes through the coloured glass.*]

Jessie, if you'll marry me I'll build you a house that soars – like this cathedral. And you, you'll give me six beautiful children, and they'll soar, mad, like that roof there. How's that?

YOUNG JESSIE: The gods'll destroy you, that's for sure.

YOUNG ANDY: Today, Jessie, I know, I know. I know everything I want to do with my life.

[*Wanders around in a trance.*

The youngsters PAUL DOBSON, STONEY JACKSON *wander in. They too have been affected by the cathedral's interior.*]

YOUNG JESSIE: I found him talking to himself.

YOUNG STONEY: And God no doubt.

YOUNG PAUL: It's that roof. The audacity, the cheek, to build like this.

YOUNG STONEY: Blessed. They were blessed.

YOUNG PAUL: Blessed? The men who built this? Never! Blasphemous, more like. To try to reach your God with pillars like these – blasphemous. Bless 'em.

YOUNG ANDY: Supposing you had the chance to build a city, a new one, all the money in the world, supposing that; this new city – what would you do with it?

YOUNG STONEY: He's off.

YOUNG ANDY: What would you chuck out, have done with?

YOUNG PAUL: Just look at it, man. Don't question, look.

YOUNG ANDY: The chance to change the pattern of living for all time? There it is, all virgin, new land, lovely, green, rich, what would we do with it? Supposing that? What would us do?

YOUNG STONEY: I wouldn't. I wouldn't even bother to answer 'cos I'd know the money would never be there.

YOUNG JESSIE: But if it were?

YOUNG STONEY: Trust you to encourage him.

YOUNG PAUL: Why not? Supposing. All these people, pooling their money, for a city, just supposing.

YOUNG STONEY: You suppose, I can't.

YOUNG JESSIE: Well, what would us do?

YOUNG STONEY: You don't expect answers, do you?

YOUNG ANDY: Did you know people thought the invention of the printing press was just a new technique for producing books?

YOUNG STONEY: He's off again.

YOUNG JESSIE: Wasn't it?

YOUNG ANDY: Was it, hell! 'Is that you up there, God?' we yelled. And presto! A thousand books came out. 'No,' they said.

YOUNG STONEY: Andy!

YOUNG ANDY: 'No.' Presto like that.

YOUNG JESSIE: But everyone knows it.

YOUNG ANDY: They don't, they don't. Aye, they know they can read a book on any subject under the sun, that they know. But it's more, the printing press meant more. It meant something could be done which a long time ago couldn't be done, change! That's what the printing press meant – change.

YOUNG STONEY: Change! Change! You always want to be changing things.

YOUNG ANDY: No! I just want to know, all the time, that change is possible. Then, when it's needed, I'll do it. STAND CLEAR.

[ANDY *stands on his head.*]

YOUNG JESSIE: Get up, you idiot, someone'll see you.

YOUNG ANDY [*still on his head*]: Stoney, you're sulkin'. [*Returns to crouching position.*] Don't sulk, Stoney. A thousand books said 'no', honest they did.

YOUNG STONEY: And another thousand said 'yes'.

YOUNG ANDY: Stoney, I love you, I don't have to love God also, do I? Kiss me. [*No response.*] I'll kiss you then. [*Gives* STONEY *a long kiss then immediately stands on his head again.*] You know, it's almost as impressive this end up.

YOUNG JESSIE: You ragged-arsed apprentice, this cathedral's done things to you.

YOUNG ANDY: Perhaps they should build them upside down.

YOUNG JESSIE: Get back, I tell you, they'll throw us out. Paul, Stoney – do something, tell him.

YOUNG STONEY: Leave him, he looks prettier.

[STONEY *wanders off to start his sketching.*]

YOUNG ANDY [*descending to crouching position again*]: And when I'm older I'll meet someone who's educated, and he'll look at me 'cos I've got an interesting face and we'll talk together and he'll think – 'this lad's not like the others, I think I can do something with him' – and we'll have long discussions – STAND CLEAR. [*Returns to standing on his head.*]

YOUNG JESSIE: Get off your head, Andy, stand on your feet.

YOUNG PAUL: You won't control him.

[PAUL *wanders off to start his sketching.*]

YOUNG JESSIE: ANDREW COBHAM!

YOUNG ANDY: I'll meet all sorts of people, learn all sorts of things – I'll have good friends, Jessie Sutherland, good people, all of them. [*Returns to his feet.*]

YOUNG JESSIE: That's better. I wonder you've any blood left in your feet. Now what are you doing? Why are you limping?

[ANDY *moves to unwrap his board and pencils.*]

YOUNG ANDY: Broke me leg down a mine.

YOUNG JESSIE: You've never been down a mine.

YOUNG ANDY: Look at that mad roof, Jessie – that's the height a man is, a house should be built that high. [*He sits, leans against wall, begins to draw.*]

YOUNG JESSIE: Does Mr Casper know that you're studying architecture out of office hours?

YOUNG ANDY: He knows.

YOUNG JESSIE: Isn't he impressed?

YOUNG ANDY: Why should he be, he doesn't believe I'll succeed.

YOUNG JESSIE: Will you though?

YOUNG ANDY: I should be in college, studying, full time.

YOUNG JESSIE: Succeed – will you?

YOUNG ANDY: But what's a poor lad to do without cash?

YOUNG JESSIE: I'm asking you, will you though?

YOUNG ANDY: Instead, I am suffering.

YOUNG JESSIE: Thee? Suffer? Tha'll never suffer, tha's too cheeky.

YOUNG ANDY: Aye, I'll succeed. I'll end up architecting. You know it in a place like this.

YOUNG JESSIE [*sitting beside him to begin her own sketching*]: How sure you sound.

[*Now the next scene slowly revolves into position with* CASPER *echoing what* YOUNG ANDREW *forecasts he will say:* 'You're a draughtsman', *etc.*]

YOUNG ANDY: Old Casper will totter around mumbling to himself, 'You're a draughtsman, a good draughtsman, good draughtsmen can't be found every day, be satisfied, the good Lord made you a draughtsman don't argue with him.' And then the news will come through that I've passed and he'll go on mumbling, 'brilliant, clever boy, the good Lord's made you an architect, praise Him then, mumble, mumble, mumble.' And he'll offer me a partnership, you'll see – dear God, look how that ceiling soars.

[*The youngsters remain.*]

SCENE TWO

It is the year 1933.
Architect's Office.
JOHN CASPER, *head of the firm, is in his office with* ANDY.
CASPER *is unfolding over a blackboard some of his favourite designs.*

CASPER: Soar! Soar! Every building doesn't have to soar, Mr Cobham. Williamson was a great architect. The good Lord made him a great architect to build modest churches not edifices of megalomania. I sometimes think you must suffer from megalomania.

ANDY: Don't stop, Mr Casper. Jessie promised to ring the examination results through soon.

CASPER: I must be quite mad doing this for you, Cobham. It's most irresponsible of me to encourage you in this wish to be an architect. You're a draughtsman, a good draughtsman, be satisfied that the good Lord – with my help – made you a draughtsman. Besides, I'm sure the normal routine of this office would have taken your mind off your results just as well.

ANDY: Jessie promised, Mr Casper, and I've never asked you to show me your favourites before – it'll be soon.

CASPER: And surely you've gathered my tastes after five years working with me?

ANDY: Just occupy me a little longer.

CASPER: This is perhaps my favourite – John Martin's alms-houses for the old people in Cirencester. Lovely houses, beautiful square – look at those gardens –

ANDY: Was it the good Lord made those or John Martin?

CASPER: Now you mock me, Cobham.

ANDY: Nay, I'm jesting, tha's a gentle man, I'd never mock thee.
    [*The phone rings.*]

CASPER: Thank God, now perhaps I can get my work done.

ANDY [*lifts phone, listens, is stunned*]: Thank you. [*Pause.*] Yes – I can hear you. [*Replaces receiver. Silence.*]

CASPER: You haven't passed. You *have* passed? They've accepted your designs? Andy lad? Look at him, has the good Lord struck you dumb? You've passed?

[ANDY *can only smile.*]

You have passed then. Well then, well I never then. The good Lord *has* made you an architect – well then. It says a lot about me, doesn't it, lad? I must see those designs again, where are they, those 'testimonies of study'? [*Looks.*] These them? [*Unfolds plans.*] Soar? Soar? Is this what you mean by soar? Yes, well it says a lot about me then.

[CASPER *lays down plans, walks once round the still silent ANDREW, then faces him, stretches out his arms and embraces him.*]

You must register with the Council of Architects, you must qualify, straight away you must do it, now to begin with, at once and then, Andrew, I'll make an offer – listen to me, talking of offers so soon, it's indecent – never mind, I'm delighted, delighted. Chief Assistant, share of the profits and promise of a partnership in two years if all goes well. What do you say? I'll ring up my solicitors now, this minute, draw up a contract, are you listening? Do you hear me? Cobham! Andrew! What are you doing? The blood'll run to your head, Andrew –

[ANDY *stands on his head and the scene has changed to –*]

SCENE THREE

A riverside, some hours later.
ANDY *still on his head.*[*]
JESSIE *packing away a picnic spread out on a groundsheet.*

ANDY: 'I'll ring up my solicitors, now, this minute,' he said, 'draw up a contract, share of the profits, a partnership –'

YOUNG JESSIE: Andy Cobham, stand on your feet, you're a big lad now.

JESSIE: What did you say?

---

*Note: YOUNG ANDY also stands on his head so that both YOUNG and OLD JESSIE say together, 'Andy Cobham, stand on your feet'. Similar links can be found throughout the play.

ANDY [*returning to his feet*]. Casper's a good man, a gentle man, but he's a dull architect. I'll not stay with him.

JESSIE: Whose practice will you join then?

ANDY: I shan't join a practice. I'll join the local Council, gain more experience.

JESSIE: What do they pay?

ANDY: Pay?

JESSIE: Are we to live on nothing when we marry?

ANDY: Oh aye – marry.

JESSIE: Look how your moods change. What is it now, Andy? [*Silence.*] Andy, I'm asking you. Sometimes I have to squeeze words from you – Andy.

ANDY: Can you feel the sun on you, Jessie? Take off your blouse.

JESSIE: Don't be mad – on a common field – to take off – undress – don't be mad.

ANDY: It's all happened with too much ease, Jessie, not much struggle.

JESSIE: Not much struggle? You! You lap up action like a kitten with milk – you wouldn't know you'd struggled till you died.

ANDY: The year of depression for everyone else but the world's going right for me.

JESSIE: Depression! Hitler! All my father does is talk of depressions and wars near by and round corners and on horizons.

ANDY: Your father's not a fool, then, he's heard the news. Terrible news, all over Europe, Jessie. Hard to believe with the sun on your back.

JESSIE: Will there be bombs, then, and killing, and destruction?

ANDY: Destruction? Aye, the cities will fall.

JESSIE: You frighten me, Andy.

ANDY [*snatching her up and hugging her*]: I want six children from you, Jessie. One after another, six of them.

JESSIE: Mind me, Andy, you're hurting me – Andy!

ANDY [*rocking her in his arms*]: Andy, Andy, chocolate pandy, that's what my kids will say, with buttons and beans and cabbage greens and rainbows every day. Jessie, it's very cold being young, isn't it, lass?

[*Suddenly* ANDY *hoists her over his shoulder.*]

Give me twelve children, twenty children –

JESSIE: Put me down, you bullying oaf, put me down, I'm feeling sick. Put me down or there'll be no children, you're pushing my belly in –

ANDY [*jumping*]: – and in and in and in and in. [*Changes her position into his arms.*] Who wants a girl more complicated than you? You're simple like a cottage loaf and pure-smelling like a rose.

JESSIE [*pushing him away*]: Simple! Simple! Cottage loaves and apple dumplings! You don't think me foolish by any chance? I mean I'd not be happy knowing we were married just 'cos we've been together these years. You wouldn't marry anyone you thought a fool – you wouldn't, would you, would you, Andy?

[*Shrouding her in a groundsheet. Now a game they play.*]

ANDY: Do you love me?

JESSIE: I love you.

ANDY: How do you know?

JESSIE: Because I love myself.

ANDY: That's a terrible conceit.

JESSIE: Conceit? But you taught me. Love yourself and you love the world. Well, I'm full of myself. I feel beautiful. Every bit of me. Look. [*Her arms stretched out wide.*] Isn't every bit of me the most beautiful thing you've ever seen? Cottage loaves, dumplings, roses and all?

[*She closes her eyes to bask in the warmth of the sun and his gaze. But her innocence and hope remind him all the more of other fears. He moves away.*]

Now look, you've changed again. You see, you change from mood to mood at such a speed.

ANDY: It's just – I'm thinking that near by it sounds like such a dreadful war that all I want to do is eat the cottage loaf and smell the rose. You've a lovely face, Jessie, lovely, lovely, lovely.

JESSIE: Catch me then.

[JESSIE *picks up picnic satchel and runs.*]

[*Off.*] Catch me, catch me. [*Silence.*] I've found another spot – the ground is softer – Andeeeeeee catch meeeeee.

[ANDY *remains. As the scene is changing* YOUNG ANDY *and* JESSIE, *arms round each other's waist, are moving off to another part of the cathedral.*]

YOUNG ANDY: And when I'm older I'll meet someone who's educated, and he'll look at me 'cos I've got an interesting face and we'll talk together and he'll think 'this lad's not like the others, I think I can do something with him' and we'll have long discussions, about all sorts of things, and I'll meet all sorts of people and learn from them. Good friends! I'll have good friends, Jessie Sutherland, good people, all of them.

[*By which time the next scene is in position.*]

SCENE FOUR

Some months later.
A public house.
A group of seven people, JAKE LATHAM, SMITHY, ANDREW COBHAM, *three union members and a* BARMAN *have gathered after a trade union branch meeting.*

SMITHY: To our retiring chairman, a toast. Jake Latham.

[*All raise glasses.*]

JAKE: My last term as chairman of the Durham Tanners' Union and only six members turned up. Even my resolution was defeated. Pathetic, isn't it? Three officials, three members and one of them is new – and our books show a membership of 259.

SMITHY: Bloody trade union branch meeting? Funeral parlour more like – where no one liked the dead 'un.

JAKE: Nineteen thirty-three will go down as one of the blackest years – I'll never understand.

SMITHY: Well you was daft to try passing a resolution on education with only a few of us here. And besides, you can't ask us to support the spending of money on education when there's no houses.

JAKE: I'm too old for your slogans about empty stomachs, Smithy, what about empty heads? Look at us. We might just as well have had the whole branch meeting in the pub.

SMITHY: Give us a farewell speech, Jake. Say something.

JAKE: Goodbye.

SMITHY: Don't be mean.

JAKE: You mean I've got to return something for this dreary old medal of service? [*Holding up watch on chain.*] I'd have done better to have stayed making saddles for the gentry! All right, I'll ask a question then. I know it's answers the young always want but I'm afraid this old 'un's going to be different – that's my reputation anyway, being different, a stale sort of reputation I'm feeling now. I haven't got answers so let's bequeath them a question eh, young Cobham? What holds a movement together? Any movement, not

even a movement, a group of people, say, or a family, or a nation
or a civilization? Something must. Do you know? Or you? Or
you? Whatever it is *we* didn't find it, God help us, *we* didn't find
it.

It's a lousy year, 1933, I don't like it at all, a miserable year in
which to end office. Gentlemen, here's to you.

[JAKE *breaks away to join* ANDY.] If you want apologies for
my morbidity you won't get it.

ANDY: I'm not afraid of a challenge.

JAKE: Challenge, is it? An optimist, are you?

ANDY: An optimist? Yes brother, I suppose I am.

JAKE: Brother! Well, I mayn't ever have the opportunity to temper
your optimism but I can advise you to drop the jargon. 'Brother!'
A useless title, full of empty love.

ANDY: A traditional greeting, Mr Latham; it's got a good history.

JAKE: Use history, don't imitate it. 'Brother' 'let's face facts!' 'Let us
stand together!' 'It's only with strong determination that we can go
forward!' Jargon!

ANDY: If the old words are failing us then perhaps they'd better be
rescued, not abandoned.

JAKE: Nonsense! You can't rescue jargon. It's the language of the
dead. Don't damn new thoughts with dead words.

ANDY: You prefer homely maxims to jargon, is it?

JAKE: That was not a homely maxim and don't be cheeky.

ANDY: Don't be —?

JAKE: — cheeky. I'm a clever man, Mr Cobham, but I'm an old and
vain one. I could teach you a lot but I can't bear a young 'un who
doesn't know his place.

ANDY: Know his —?

JAKE: — place. Stop gawping — you'll get lockjaw. I've no time for
rebels, they hate the past for what it didn't give them. The Labour
Movement is choked with bad-mannered, arrogant little rebels who
enjoy kicking stubborn parents in the teeth. Revolutionaries is what
we want — they spend less time rebelling against what's past and
give their energy to the vision ahead.

ANDY: 'The vision ahead?' I thought that was the jargon we should
drop, Mr Latham.

JAKE: Oh ye gods! Good night, Mr Cobham. [*Makes to go.*]

ANDY: Jake Latham!

[JAKE *stops*.]
What could you teach me?
[JAKE *pauses to assess this young man as the scene revolves to*]

SCENE FIVE

JAKE's *study, some weeks later.* ANDY *is helping* JAKE *rearrange his bookcase.*

JAKE: When you come to me and say 'teach me' what do you mean? No, first – why me?

ANDY: I've always had a picture in my mind of an old, sorry –

JAKE: Yes, yes, old, I'm old, don't fumble, I'm old.

ANDY: A man, somebody, who'd talk to me. Don't misunderstand me, I don't want to be told what to think. I've read, I've always read, but I've never been, well, guided. Waste, I can't bear waste. I may die young, you see.

JAKE: Huh! romantic as well. An optimistic romantic! I'd say you were doomed, Cobham. Go home.

ANDY: I'm not impressed with cynicism, Mr Latham, it's a bit dull is cynicism. You say I'm damned and it sounds clever I know, but I'm not impressed. Neither were you, were you?

JAKE: Are you patronizing me, young lad, are you?

ANDY: Mr Latham, I –

JAKE: I've been chairman of my branch, Cobham, on and off for the last twenty years, chairman of a local trade union branch in a dreadful and dreary industrial town. Does it occur to you to ask why someone like me is a chairman only of a local branch – does it?

ANDY: Perhaps you'll tell me in good time but just now –

JAKE: Right! Learn? You want to learn? Answer me this then. Ramsay MacDonald handed in his resignation as Labour Prime Minister two years ago and assumed the Leadership of a National Coalition Government. What led up to that 1931 crisis?

ANDY: I work in an architect's office, Mr Latham, I want to build cities, I'm not a student of economics.

JAKE: How interesting. You want to build cities but you don't want to know about economics.

ANDY: Do I have to know about economics before I'm permitted to build my cities?

JAKE: Your cities, eh?

ANDY: Why laugh at me? Is it every day someone comes to you and says 'teach me'?

JAKE: No. Never, actually. No one's ever given me such a responsibility. Laugh, do I? Daft old man, me. I'm a bit overwhelmed perhaps. I don't know what to teach you, lad. It must have been the vanity of an old man made me invite you here. I'm not a teacher. I've got a pocket full of principles, that's all really. If you'd tried to answer my question I'd have tried to apply those principles, but . . . There *was* a principle involved in that crisis you know. It wasn't very widely argued but it was there. Do you know what the Bank of England did – poor bloody Ramsay MacDonald – they frightened the pants off him. All our gold was going, you see, flowing out of the window it was, people drawing left, right and centre. So the directors of the Bank demanded to see the Prime Minister and give him their view of the situation. And what was their view? They said to him: 'MacDonald, old son, this isn't a financial problem, it's a political one. No one abroad will lend us any money because they are worried about your government,' they said. 'The Labour Government is squandering,' they said, 'too much money on silly things, frivolous things, social services and education,' they said. 'Foreigners don't trust your government, Mr MacDonald, they don't think you can handle the affairs of the British nation.' Huh! You wouldn't think that a Labour Prime Minister would fall for anything as simple as that, would you? But he did, old MacDonald. 'You're right,' he said to the Bank of England. 'We *have* been silly, I'll make cuts.' So he tried, but he didn't have all the Cabinet with him, and he resigned, formed a coalition government and then made the cuts. It's almost unbelievable, isn't it? Where does the principle come in? I'll tell you. [*Beginning to get excited.*] Would it have been unreasonable to expect a socialist government to apply socialist economic principles instead of the usual patchwork? It wouldn't, would it? But did they? [*Mocking.*] 'The time isn't ripe! The government'll be defeated!' The sort of answer we all give when we don't do the things we feel are right. So here's the question: is it better to risk defeat in defence of a principle or hang on with compromises?

ANDY [*eagerly, infected by* JAKE's *excitement*]: Do you want me to answer?

JAKE: Of course not, just listen. Now, er, where was I?

ANDY: Compromise!

JAKE: Ah! Now, people always need to know that someone was around who acted. Defeat doesn't matter; in the long run all defeat is temporary. It doesn't matter about present generations but future ones always want to look back and know that someone was around acting on principle. That government, I tell you, should've screamed out to the opposition 'REVOLUTION' – like that. 'Control imports! Clamp down on speculators! Revolution!' Like that, at the top of its voice; and then, taken hold of British industry by the scruff of its neck and made it develop, themselves, full employment! And perhaps they'd have crashed – it was a doomed government anyway – and perhaps we'd have shuddered. But after the crash, after the shuddering and the self-pitying and the recriminations, we'd have been stunned with admiration and the sounds of the crash would've echoed like bloody great hallelujahs, bloody great hallelujahs – What the hell you standing on your head for? You silly or something? Apoplectic?

ANDY: It's relaxing, I'm happy.

JAKE: You're a vegetarian also, I suppose?

ANDY: Here, you try it.

JAKE: Me?

ANDY: I'll make it easy for you. [*Lies on his back and raises his knees.*] Put your hands on my knees.

JAKE: Certainly not.

ANDY: You're so dull, you politicians. I'll catch you.

[KATHERINE RAMSAY *enters.*]

KATE: How amusing, Jake.

JAKE: Andrew Cobham, this is Katherine Ramsay; Kate – Andrew Cobham.

ANDY [*jumping up*]: I didn't know you were expecting a visitor. [*To* KATE.] Evening.

JAKE: Sit down, boy, I've invited her so that you two could meet. Kate is the daughter of Lord and Lady Ramsay – the local landlords. Her mother and I were once er – well, as a young man I worked for her father, as a saddler, and she and I – once, er, well, we were in love.

KATE: You can almost see him stiffen, Jake.

JAKE: No, she's not my daughter.

KATE: I thought you said he was different.

JAKE: Beautiful woman – Kate's mum – rare, strong. Great scandal! And my puritanical colleagues never let me forget it. Thank God I'm also a good organizer.

KATE: You're a draughtsman, Mr –

ANDY: Cobham's the name.

[ANDY *attempts to leave.*]

JAKE: What you rushing for?

ANDY: My fiancée – I'm meeting her.

KATE: Why do you limp, Mr –?

ANDY: Cobham's the name.

JAKE: Why does he what?

ANDY: I used to be a miner, Miss, and one day the props gave way and I used my leg instead – for five hours till help came. I've not been able to use it since.

KATE: But you –

ANDY: Good night, then, glad to have met you, Miss – er – Kate.

KATE: Kate!

ANDY: Thank you, Jake.

[ANDY *goes, limping badly and bravely into his bedsitter which is revolving into view**]

JAKE: Mine? He's never been near a mine.

JAKE: Of course not, Jake, he's never been near a mine.

SCENE SIX

ANDY's *bedsitter, some days later.* KATE *enters.*

ANDY *is at work on his drawing board.* KATE *nonchalantly sorts through his books.*

KATE: Why did you run away from Jake's that night?

ANDY: You're a forward lass, coming upon me like this.

*Note: At the same time JAKE and his study are being revolved off stage. KATE has to walk forward into the new set/scene.

It will be obvious by now how these changes are effected, and from here on such stage directions will be omitted.

JAKE: Were you afraid?

ANDY: How did you know I'd be in?

KATE: It's my nature to take chances. Were you afraid?

ANDY: I bet you smoke pipes.

KATE: No, cigars. Were you afraid?

ANDY: I try not to be feared of anything.

KATE: Why did you go so quickly then?

ANDY: How you do persist.

KATE: Persistence is a family trait. You turned on your heel because my mother is Lady Ramsay, didn't you? I want you to know, Mr Cobham, I'm a classless woman.

ANDY: Aye, I can see it.

KATE: I can't bear people who wear their class on their hearts like an emblem.

ANDY: Seems to me you're more intent in denying it than I am in looking for it.

KATE: I want us to be friends.

ANDY: You sound desperate.

KATE: Passionate, not desperate. You must know certain things about me, Mr Cobham.

ANDY: I don't see as I must know anything. I was brought up to earn friendship.

KATE: That's our difference then, I don't have to earn anything, I was born with rights.

ANDY: Aye, of course, you're a classless woman.

KATE [attempting to fold his pile of unpressed clothes]: You're a fool if you think I'm talking about class rights. [He snatches shirt from her hands. She gently retrieves it and continues folding.] Human rights, Mr Cobham, from any class. There are certain people who are born with natures that naturally deserve love and respect. Yours, like mine, is one of them.

ANDY: I think you're seeing me as you want.

KATE: Oh? You really see yourself as a humble man? You shame yourself with false modesty?

ANDY: I don't see as how modesty is always false, and I don't see as how being capable and ambitious should make me immodest. I am what I am, I don't feel the need to boast loudly or deny loudly. What I *do* is my boast, not what I say or don't say.

KATE: Charming, Andy, it becomes you.

ANDY: And I'm not needing your comments.

KATE: Don't be ungracious.

ANDY: I'm annoyed.

KATE: Don't be annoyed either, it's my nature to be direct.

ANDY: It's your nature to be a lot of things, it seems. Do you always talk about yourself?

KATE: I want us to be friends.

ANDY: You want, you want! You'll have to earn, young lady.

[He returns to try and work. She takes out a long, thin cigar.]

KATE: How long have you lived here?

ANDY: Eighteen months.

KATE [referring to a chair]: Did you buy that monstrosity or does it belong here?

ANDY: It belongs here.

KATE: Why don't you get rid of it?

ANDY: It belongs here.

KATE: My dear, the landlady should be given to understand that you are doing her a kindness by getting rid of it.

ANDY: It's not my habit to interfere with other people's property.

KATE: And you're the socialist, are you? [He protests. She ploughs on.] Look at this room. You want to be an architect? You want to build beautiful homes? Then how can you surround yourself with ugliness? Look how you dress, look what you hang on your walls. How can you dare plan other people's houses when you live with such mediocrity?

ANDY: I –

KATE: How can you dare?

ANDY: I –

KATE: How?

ANDY: I – blast you, woman, I'll not have anyone talk at me like this.

KATE: Honesty hurts you, then?

ANDY: It's your tone of voice, it gets in the way.

KATE: Do you deny that I'm right?

ANDY: I'll not be dragged –

KATE: You deny I'm right?

ANDY: I'll not –

KATE: Do you?

ANDY: I'm attached to my surroundings. Personal things count for me. That's a truth also – attachments count.

KATE: Even attachments to the third-rate?

[*Pause.*]

ANDY: You know, I'd agree with you if only your voice didn't sneer at your words. I don't like people who sneer.

[*She offers him a lovely smile.*]

KATE: Tell me, have you ever really worked down a mine?

ANDY: No.

KATE: Why did you limp, then?

ANDY: It's a joke I have.

KATE: Why look, you're blushing.

ANDY: Ye gods, has ever a person so twisted me all ways in so short a time?

KATE: What is the joke?

ANDY: It's a silly joke.

KATE: Tell it me.

[*Music. Tallis.*

As they are moved off she is smiling at his confusion and embarrassment through which his own smile breaks. They will be friends for life.]

SCENE SEVEN

The Cathedral.
Music continuing. The young ones are all sitting eating sandwiches.

YOUNG STONEY: How will we really all end, I wonder? Will we stay the friends we are?

YOUNG ANDY: I remember at school we used to ask, 'Where shall us be in five years from now – just five years?'

YOUNG PAUL [*croaking*]: Five years older.

YOUNG STONEY: I've tomato sandwiches – who likes tomato sandwiches?

YOUNG JESSIE: I'll swop half a pork pie for two of them.

YOUNG STONEY: Don't like pork pies – they're all fat.

YOUNG JESSIE: I made it myself.

[PAUL *starts coughing.*]

YOUNG ANDY: Shut up coughing, Paul, and read us one of your poems.

YOUNG STONEY: Why do all poets die of consumption?

YOUNG JESSIE: Give over, Stoney – the air here is none too good for a cough like that.

YOUNG STONEY: She doesn't speak much but when she does – what wisdom.

YOUNG JESSIE: The gift for gabbing belongs to you, it's you who's taking up religion.

YOUNG ANDY: Stoney Jackson will be the most irreverent priest I know.

YOUNG PAUL [looking at one scrap of paper]:
'My lids lay heavily with guilt . . .'
No, not that one. [Searching through other scraps.]

> You love me now but wait until
> Upon my lips you feed no more
> And in my arms you lie and scatter
> Lovely dreams you struggled for.
> Upon my heart you'll lay your head
> And know of things that matter more.
>
> So hard is love and soft its sighs
> And soft the contours of our lives,
> Not all your woman's winter tears
> Shall take you back among sweet sighs.
> You love me now but wait until
> You've crossed my love between your thighs.

[There is a long silence. Music, the poem, youthful friendship have drawn them together. YOUNG ANDY, moved, leaps up hugging himself with pleasure.]

YOUNG JESSIE: You were a gang when I first met you all.

YOUNG ANDY [sauntering around in his own world]: There's something about people getting together and doing things.

YOUNG JESSIE: You were all in Woolworth's together.

YOUNG ANDY: I don't see the point of insisting you're an individual – you're born one anyway.

YOUNG JESSIE: I was fascinated.

YOUNG ANDY: But a group together, depending on each other, knowing what they want, knowing how to get it –

YOUNG JESSIE: Stoney used to pretend he was blind, and I remember

Paul could walk from one end of the city to the other without looking up from his book.

YOUNG ANDY: But a group together —

YOUNG JESSIE: I watched you all —

YOUNG ANDY: Now that's something.

YOUNG JESSIE: You were pinching sweets.

YOUNG STONEY: Ssh!

YOUNG PAUL: What is it?

YOUNG STONEY: They've started a service.

[*Music grows.*

ANDREW *mounts the catafalque.*]

YOUNG ANDY: I'll give a sermon.

[PAUL *and* STONEY *start applauding.*]

YOUNG JESSIE: Now they'll chuck us out, now sure as sure they'll chuck us out.

YOUNG ANDY: Shut up, you ignorant proles you, don't you know you mustn't applaud in churches? Now, dearly beloved apprentices, my ragged-arsed brothers, my sermon today comes from the Bible.

YOUNG STONEY: All sermons come from the Bible.

YOUNG ANDY: Well, my Bible then. And the prophet Blake said, 'Bring me my bow of burning gold, bring me my arrows of desire.'

[YOUNG JESSIE *begins to hum the song in a softly mock heroic manner. Against her humming* ANDY *delivers his 'sermon'.*]

YOUNG STONEY: Since when did you read Blake in the Bible?

YOUNG ANDY: I didn't, I read the Bible in Blake — now hush! 'Bring me my spear, O clouds unfold, bring me my chariot of fire! I will not cease from mental strife, nor shall my sword sleep in my hand, till we have built Jerusalem in England's green and pleasant land.' Till we have built Jerusalem, dearly beloved apprentices, in England's green and pleasant land. Now, how can we build Jerusalem in England's green and pleasant land?

ALL: Get rid of the rotten houses!

YOUNG ANDY: Right. Who built the rotten houses?

ALL: The property owners!

YOUNG ANDY: Right. Who's going to kick the property owners out?

ALL: Labour!

YOUNG ANDY: Right. Who's going to control the next government?

ALL: Labour!

YOUNG ANDY: Right. And —

YOUNG JESSIE: Quick, there's someone coming.

[ANDY *scampers down and everyone innocently turns to his sketching board. A* FROCKED PRIEST *walks through, smiling encouragingly at them.* ANDY *resumes his sermon, but not from the tomb.*]

YOUNG ANDY: And when the new Labour comes, who will they turn to to build their homes?

ALL: Us!

YOUNG ANDY: 'Boys', they'll say, no, 'Sons' – 'sons', that's what they'll call us. 'Our sons,' they'll say. 'We've done it, we won, now – to work, you ragged-arsed brothers. Build us homes.' That's what they'll say – 'Build us homes' – am I right, boys?

[*They all get ready to go back to their drawing.*]

YOUNG PAUL: You're right –

YOUNG STONEY: Of course he's right –

YOUNG ANDY: Of course I'm right!

YOUNG PAUL [*going off*]: He's always right!

YOUNG STONEY [*much too loudly*]: He's always right!

YOUNG JESSIE and ANDY [*together*]: Ssssh!

YOUNG STONEY [*wandering off in another direction, clumsily, thinking – as always – that he's forgotten something*]: Ssssh!

[YOUNG ANDY *and* JESSIE *skip off hand in hand jubilantly chanting 'New Labour! New Labour! New Labour!'*]

SCENE EIGHT

The riverside. It is the year 1935.

KATE *and* ANDY *approaching.*

ANDY: New Labour! New Labour! We never learn, never!

KATE: I take it you're having housing problems with the local council.

ANDY [*laying out raincoat for her*]: Patchwork, patchwork. It's like Jake says – they do nothing but patchwork.

KATE [*lying down*]: What do you expect from clerks and butchers?

ANDY: Beware, beware, my brethren, of the woman who claims to be classless.

KATE: There's not even a dignified pause and 'bang' – look at your emancipated working class, leaping to adopt the values of simpering shopkeepers.

ANDY: She sneers, my God, how she sneers.

KATE [*sitting up*]: Stop fighting me, Andrew Cobham, my attacks are reserved for the half-hearted and insensitive. I don't attack a class, only certain kinds of human beings. Just because the bloody town council sits on your designs. You don't like the town council? Change them! Or join them –

[*Pause.*]

Ah! Join them! Now that's an idea. Tick tick tick tick. Look at that brain turning over and over. [*Lying back again.*]

ANDY: When a person talks, I think.

KATE: Tick tick tick tick. When Jake first introduced us I said, 'Keep an eye on that young man.'

ANDY: She's talking about herself again.

KATE: Tick tick tick tick. He will play his life like a game of chess, Jake, I said. Working ten moves ahead – a politician's way, really. But I suppose one will admire him, I said, for being a gambler – because if the first move is wrong he's gambled away the next nine.

ANDY: How clever the young Ramsay girl is, so observant about people, so witty and naughty.

KATE: Tick tick tick tick. How's your wife?

ANDY: We used to court here, by this river – the 'smelly'.

KATE: A clever girl that, her head screwed on.

ANDY [*taking off socks and shoes*]: Our womenfolk aren't social plotters, you know – not calculating, like your lot.

KATE: Nonsense! A woman will calculate no matter which class she comes from – or would you like to sell me the myth of the working-class mother tending her brood of hard-working sons and plain-speaking daughters?

ANDY: How cool the grass is.

KATE: Still, I suppose it's good for the biography. Andrew Cobham, a man of simple tastes – great though he was he constantly returned to the bosom of the common people and his simple wife.

ANDY: My house is in order, my food is cooked, and my children are loved and cared for.

KATE: Yes, well, it sounds as though you have a good housekeeper. Only she sent you out with a button missing from your shirt. Our housekeeper wouldn't put anything back in the drawer without looking for tears and lost buttons.

ANDY: I'm sure that when the costume you're wearing loses its buttons you'll just buy a new one.

KATE: I didn't buy this one, I made it.

ANDY: You have hobbies then – how clever.

KATE: Not clever at all – I hate making things. If I had my way I'd have everything made for me, I can't bear manual labour, but it relieves my boredom and softens my temper.

ANDY: Are you in love with me?

KATE: Yes.

ANDY: God knows why I asked. [*Pause.*] Now look at that city down there. What gangrenous vision excited the men who built that, I wonder?

KATE: There's a war coming, soon.

ANDY: Soon?

KATE: Two or three years.

ANDY: That soon?

KATE: Unless I've drawn the wrong conclusions from what I saw.

ANDY: You really went in cold blood, parading as a Nazi sympathizer, admiring the work of concentration camps?

KATE: What matter how cold my blood was? I needed to know. I told them I was a journalist and went to find out.

ANDY: You're a ruthless woman, Kate Ramsay.

KATE: Oh you're such a bore with your half-hearted humanity. Ruthless! My so-called ruthlessness has now equipped me to save thousands. [*Pause. Unable to resist pricking him.*] Besides, can I help it if I look like the master race?

ANDY: I don't know why we fought for sex equality, so help me I don't.

KATE: Rest on no laurels, my dear, it hasn't happened yet. Do you know I once asked Jake to take me to his union branch meeting and he spent all evening with his tail between his legs – I embarrassed him.

ANDY: Dressed with your sort of ostentatiously simple elegance, I don't wonder.

KATE [*rising*]: Simple elegance is not ostentatious – unless you're not used to it. Or would you have me go to his branch meeting dressed in tweeds or those nasty cotton frocks from the stores? I don't believe in wearing cloth caps to earn love from the masses. [*Pause.*] Andy – would you consider standing for councillor?

ANDY: If only you didn't make politics sound like a dirty job.

KATE: How touchy he is.

ANDY: What the hell do I know of local politics?

KATE: You could get in — you're trusted.

ANDY [*moving off*]: God help me, Kate, I don't want to go into local politics — I'm an architect; they should be screaming for me to build their houses, down on their bloody knees for me.

KATE [*following*]: Singing hallelujahs for you.

ANDY: Aye, well, aye! Singing hallelujahs for me.

    [*They've gone.*]

SCENE NINE

Andy's study. It is the year 1936.

Empty.

STONEY *staggers in pretending to be blind.* JESSIE *follows him with a tea tray.*

STONEY: Where is he, where's the man? Take me to him, let me feel him. [*Feels a chair.*] Andy? Ah master, safe and sound, still with us. God be praised.

JESSIE: Stoney Jackson! You're the most irreverent priest I know. God'll have stern things to tell thee, lad.

STONEY: He's still got his wooden leg.

JESSIE: Get off your knees, fool — your childhood's passed.

    [PAUL *enters.*]

PAUL: Is the reverend bloody father still playing games?

    [PAUL *and* STONEY *help themselves to tea, they are 'at home'.*]

STONEY: Is Andy still with the council?

PAUL: How long does a council meeting go on for, for God's sake?

JESSIE: You should know, Paul, you've covered them often enough.

PAUL: Is he going to stand for council again?

JESSIE: No, he's not. He'll finish this term of office and then go into practice on his own. Two minor building projects is all he's pushed through and he says it's not worth it.

PAUL: I see they're writing about his schemes in the *Architects' Journal*.

JESSIE: That's what you're here to talk about.

STONEY: Aye, Andy and his cities; we've been summoned.

JESSIE: That's right, boys, you've been summoned. He has his answers.

[*The men surprise* JESSIE *by hoisting her on their shoulders, as though back to their youth. But she accepts her place as 'Queen', folding her arms regally.*]

STONEY [*quoting Andy*]: 'What would you chuck out, have done with? What new things would you put there?'

PAUL: 'There it is, all virgin, a new piece of land, lovely, green, rich, what would us do with it?'

STONEY: 'Private industry? Have done with it. Let the unions and the co-ops take over – think what we could do with the profits.'

PAUL: 'Politicians are men we hire to mend roads and tend to the sewers.'

STONEY: 'The Prime Minister is an accountant. Give the city to its teachers and artists.'

JESSIE: He has his answers.

[*With great laughter they lower her.*]

STONEY: Aye, we know them.

[*Sounds of* ANDY *approaching and arguing with someone else. It is* SMITHY, *chairman of the local Labour Party.*]

SMITHY: And you must debate it, Andy, you, in public, and you know it.

PAUL: What is it, Andy?

ANDY: Jake – the bloody fool.

PAUL: What is it?

SMITHY: I'm chairman of this city's Labour Party –

PAUL: Aye –

SMITHY: Thirty years in the movement.

PAUL: Aye, aye.

SMITHY: I've seen it before –

PAUL: Will you give over rambling and –

SMITHY: If I ramble, Paul, then that's my pace, let me make my own pace. It may be slow and maybe I'm not as brilliant as some of you, but my political experience tells me no one'll follow a divided party.

PAUL: What's agitating him, Andy?

SMITHY: Local elections, that's what's agitating me. Next week we've got local elections and in a year's time general elections and Jake Latham's splitting the party.

PAUL: Smithy –

SMITHY: At my own pace, Paul, please, at my own pace. Labour Party Conference last year voted to re-arm and give more power to the League of Nations so's the Nazis could be prevented from growing – right? And now there's a split in the party and Jake is among those who've turned against the party's decision to support economic sanctions and re-armament.

PAUL: Against?

SMITHY: Alright, we all know it might lead to war, but the party's decision was a responsible one.

PAUL: Against? On the eve of elections?

SMITHY: Who'll vote for us now? Thirty years in the movement – split after split – a party of individuals and eccentrics. Everyone shooting their mouths off in different directions. Bloody intellectuals!

STONEY: Well, Andy?

SMITHY: No discipline, that's what I can't understand, no discipline.

STONEY: Politics is your game now – here's your first big dilemma: eve of poll and your closest friend has decided to take a stand on his own.

SMITHY: He can take whatever stand he likes but not after he's allowed policy to be made, not after he's continued to stand as Area Chairman on that policy. [*Pause.*] Andy, you – you must argue it out, at the next meeting, with Jake, before the elections, I'll get every delegate to pack the hall.

PAUL: Don't be a fool, Smithy – you can't ask Andy to attack Jake in public, not old friends you can't.

SMITHY: Old friends, old friends! We're all old friends, sloppy bloody old friends. The movement can burn and you wouldn't care so long as we was old friends together.

ANDY: I'll talk to him.

SMITHY: No Andy. I want it debated. I'm in the chair and I'll see –

ANDY: I'll talk to him, I tell you.

STONEY: And your plans, Andy? For the new cities? Your answers?

ANDY: Aye, the new cities, well they'll have to wait. There's another bloody war coming up. They'll have to wait.

[ANDY *and a commiserating* JESSIE *go off.* YOUNG ANDY, *arm round* YOUNG JESSIE, *strolls through to take up position by catafalque. Like a reprise he tells her again:*]

YOUNG ANDY: And when I'm older I'll meet someone who's

educated, and he'll look at me 'cos I've got an interesting face and
we'll talk together and he'll think 'this lad's not like the others. I
think I can do something with him' and we'll have long discussions,
about all sorts of things and I'll meet all sorts of people and learn
from them. Good friends! I'll have good friends, Jessie Sutherland,
good people, all of them.

[*They sit back to back, as the future continues to be played out
around them.*]

SCENE TEN

ANDY's *study some days later.*
JAKE *and* ANDY.

JAKE: Perhaps I should have told you. Of all people I should have
told you.

ANDY: Fool.

JAKE: Old, Andy, I'm an old man. I don't always feel inclined to
discuss every thought.

ANDY: Then stand down, old men should stand down.

JAKE: Old men should, should they?

ANDY: Don't play with me now, Jake. Stand down.

JAKE: Old men. So we fight, do we?

ANDY: I shall state what I feel to be right.

JAKE: Oh, Andy lad, how you do sound pompous at times. You don't
have to be evasive with me. I ask you, we fight – do we?

ANDY: Hasn't Kate told you? Haven't you understood what Kate has
told you? The Nazis have burnt the books of their poets – their
poets, Jake.

JAKE: You know Kate is returning to Europe?

ANDY: I know it.

JAKE: 'I look like the master race,' she said, 'and I can speak fluent
German. No better qualifications for a secret agent, you know.'

ANDY: It'll satisfy her need for drama, she'll love it.

JAKE: What'll you do when the war is over?

ANDY: Damn the war – damn you and the war.

[*Enter* JESSIE *with clean shirt at the ready.*]

JAKE: Perhaps the war will clear a path for you – you and your cities.

ANDY: Jake, don't oppose me at the meeting.

JAKE: Don't?

ANDY: I don't want to fight my friends.

JAKE [*idly picking up a sheet of Andy's notes*]: You shouldn't saddle yourself with friends whose opinions you don't share.

ANDY: Don't oppose me, Jake, I'm weary of battling.

JAKE: Weary already?

ANDY: You don't think I enjoyed those council battles?

JAKE: It's you who should stand down perhaps.

> [ANDY *is silent*.]

> Aye, then we'll fight. It'll be a good lesson for thee. I'll not stay to tea, lass. Look after him.

> [JAKE *leaves*.]

JESSIE: You can't, Andy – not Jake. That's a long friendship.

ANDY: Why do you always remind me of the things I know?

JESSIE [*helping him into shirt*]: Here, it's pressed. I hope it's not still damp.

ANDY: Pressed? This collar? Pressed?

JESSIE: Collars are difficult, they never press straight.

ANDY: And there's a button missing. Time and again I've asked you – never put anything back without checking for tears and loose buttons. Now I shall be late.

JESSIE: There's others.

ANDY: No, I'll make do.

JESSIE [*buttoning him up while he knots his tie*]: You're snapping, Andy.

ANDY: Snap? Do I? I didn't ever think I'd be a grumpy old man.

JESSIE: Thirty – old?

ANDY: It's a bad age, thirty. At twenty-nine you're still a young man; at thirty, well, it's a halfway point between then and never.

JESSIE: I suppose everyone will be there.

ANDY: Yes.

JESSIE: Will you come back afterwards – the two of you?

ANDY: Probably.

JESSIE: Shall I make food?

ANDY: Food we'll have had. Just tea, your cake and some strong tea.

JESSIE: It won't be a vicious argument, will it, Andy?

ANDY: I shall state what I feel to be right.

JESSIE: Of course.

ANDY: You don't think that's pompous, do you; you never think anything I say is pompous – but it is. Jake's right. I never thought I'd be pompous.

JESSIE: Grumpy and pompous – all at thirty, my!

ANDY [*embracing her*]: Oh God, Jessie, shall us ever build cities? Shall us ever stop wasting energy and build those cities?

JESSIE: No time is waste, Andy.

ANDY: Yes, waste.

[*He moves to take up his position on the new set revolving in.*]

JESSIE: It's all a time of growing, lad.

ANDY: Waste.

JESSIE: Growing, growing, it's a time of growing, believe me.

ANDY: Waste! Waste! Waste!

SCENE ELEVEN

It's a large meeting, some months later. The debate is in progress. Centre is chairman, SMITHY. *Left standing forward is* JAKE, *right is* ANDY. (*Note:* The platform must *not* face the audience but should face downstage, off, from where come the intermittent sounds, growls or applause of the unseen public.)

JAKE [*emotionally*]: . . . God knows how it was done. I don't know how it was done. The degree to which we can be fooled sometimes leads me to despair and despise the class from which I come.

And now again, in 1936, the same humbugging machinery is in operation, the same appeal to our patriotism is being made. Do we sharpen our knives again? Is that our answer? Every time, is that going to be our answer? Don't you know what we've created in these last hundred years? An international movement capable of raising a finger and saying yes or no to every important issue confronting the world today.

Why did we create it? To raise our wages from one shilling to one and a penny an hour? Is that all?

[*Gentler.*] I am aware that if we do not fight this war then our civilization will enter into terrible times. Terrible times. I know this – I've not loaded the argument on my side, if anything I've done the opposite. But what can an old man do except say the things he passionately believes? Old men have no need to lie, it's all over for them – the days of tactic, of political manoeuvre, of patchwork. What should an old man say but the thoughts which all his life he's felt were perhaps too irresponsible to utter? Irresponsible? It is said that people like me are irresponsible. I don't know, my friends, I do not know. I feel I will never know the answer – your vote for my resolution calling a halt to this useless rush to re-arm must be my answer; what you decide will decide me.

But,

[*Urgently.*] I want to say this. Defeat doesn't matter. In the long run all defeat is temporary. It doesn't matter about present generations, but future ones always want to look back and know that someone was around acting on their beliefs. I can only tell you that I believe you were intended to live on this earth at peace with one another – if some people do not allow us to do this then I am ready to stand as the early Christians did and say – this is my faith, this is where I stand and if necessary, this is where I will die.

[*Tumultuous applause.*]

ANDY [*very coolly*]: Andrew Cobham, secretary Number 7 Branch. I want you to know that the man I shall be attacking is the one to whom I owe most of my intellectual development; in this way you will know how deeply I feel about the issue. This meeting must not be influenced either by sentiment or personal attachment. Let me remind you that when Jake Latham says what he has said today it is rather late to say it and I hope you will carry no resolution of an emergency character simply to help a man with a conscience like Jake's decide what he ought to do. How he should act is a matter for his own conscience. For Jake Latham to hawk his conscience around for other people to absolve is not only confusing the issue but is basically dishonest. [*Roar of disagreement.* ANDY *must fight all the way.*] Because, if in the end Jake Latham is going to act on the basis of individual conscience, then he had no right at any time to assume a position of leadership.

JAKE: I've always declared my position.

ANDY [*to* JAKE, *warm though chastising*]: But you remained in office knowing you were leading hundreds of people who in the end you would have to abandon on grounds of private conscience.

VOICES: We asked him to stay!

Thank God he did! etc.

ANDY [*back to public, contemptuously*]: You asked him to stay! You asked him to stay! For love? For affection? There was a time when you prevented this man from going to the top of his movement because of some private affair that offended your puritanical morals and now you declare love for him? Why? Because he's shaking with the pain of his own conscience? When your father has an accident do you sit and croon about your love for him or do you ignore your love and face the fact there are hospitals that can cure him? Love or facts? There is a time for love when facts are faced. This is no moment to be seated at the feet of self-styled saints.

VOICES: Shame!

Withdraw!

He's more of a saint than you'll ever be.

ANDY [*raising his voice above the cries*]: I tell you, I tell you – if you want Jake Latham to become a saint then let me make it easier for you by lighting the faggots for his martyrdom.

[*Stunned silence.* ANDY *begins at low temperature, rising to crescendo.*]

Facts. Facts. It's too late for sentiment and, just as you, I'm sick at heart that this is so.

Now,

let us begin. The argument is that this will be another war which in the end will serve the interests of those who rule.

Facts:

In every fascist state it is the Labour Movement that has been attacked; who fondly thinks that in defeat it will not happen here? The argument is for unity of Labour's International Movement to prevent this war.

Facts:

Jake Latham is the man who calls for unity, but look – he takes a stand that cracks the very solidarity he wants.

How dare he argue then for unity?

The argument is that in a war we should reply by paralysing every nation with a strike.

Facts:

Who will strike? The unions are destroyed in most of Europe. Who's left?

Confronted with these facts do we continue speaking glibly about what could be achieved by strike in the event of war? There only ever was one answer – the international control of the seas and an economic pact throughout the world which would control the source of our raw materials. That was an answer, at the time, the right time. Now, it's too late. I'm sorry, Jake Latham, saint, or no saint, it's too late. [*Out of disgust with what he's had to do he throws this last sentence away and returns to table.*] Those who can't accept the movement's policy must take a course that is their own – but not, I tell you, not inside this movement.

[*Applause, starting slowly, hesitantly mounts to huge ovation.* ANDY, JAKE *and* SMITHY *step down.* SMITHY *attempts to shake* ANDY's *hand.* ANDY *turns his back.* SMITHY *leaves.*]

ANDY: Damn you, Jake Latham, you've made me do damage to myself again.

JAKE: Did you imagine it was facts that swayed that gathering to your side, Andy? When you stand up and say you're sick at heart, you win a sentimental point and all your pleas to them to take no heed of sentiment are waste. And when you say you owe a debt to someone you attack, then you have made another sentimental point which all your pleading to ignore will not cut out. And was it fair to say I 'hawked' my conscience all around? Was that the action of a friend.

ANDY: You're saying I betrayed a friend?

JAKE: Be careful of your cities, that's what I'm saying. One day you're old and you say right things – but it's all too late; that's what I'm saying.

ANDY: Will you come back with me now? Jessie has cake and tea ready.

JAKE: Cake and strong tea, is it? Aye, let's go. I'll go with you home.

[*Arm on* ANDY's *shoulder, they leave.*
The stage slowly comes to dark. The sound of an air-raid siren is heard; planes approach, bombs fall, flames crackle – the war has come and must be past in these few seconds until –]

SCENE TWELVE

The Cathedral.
YOUNG JESSIE *heaves* YOUNG ANDY *to his feet. She is in a state of high excitement.*

YOUNG JESSIE: What kind of cities shall we build, Andy?

YOUNG ANDY: Cities of light and shade, Jessie, with secret corners.
   [YOUNG PAUL *and* STONEY *have just rushed in, in a larking mood.*]

YOUNG JESSIE: Paul, what kind of cities?

YOUNG PAUL [*getting to his knees, hands on heart*]: Cities for lovers, Jessie, and crowds and lone wolves.

YOUNG JESSIE: Stoney?

YOUNG STONEY [*croaking to his knees*]: Cities for old men and crawling children, Jessie.
   [*From their kneeling position both boys can hoist a surprised* JESSIE *on to their shoulders where she then sits as 'queen' folding her arms regally. They parade her around the stage as though showing her their cities,* YOUNG ANDY *leading.*]

YOUNG ANDY: Cosy cities, Jessie, family cities.

YOUNG PAUL: With wide streets and twisting lanes.

YOUNG STONEY: And warm houses, low arches, long alleys.

YOUNG ANDY: Cities full of sound for the blind and colour for the deaf.

YOUNG PAUL: Cities that cradle the people who live there.

YOUNG ANDY: That frighten no one.

YOUNG STONEY: That sing the praises of all men, Jessie.
   [*They pause in their marching. She rises to the mood of prophecy and catechism.*]

YOUNG JESSIE: Who will help you, my ragged-arsed brothers?

YOUNG ANDY: The new Labour!

YOUNG JESSIE: The same as asked you to build the new houses?

YOUNG ANDY: Aye. After we've built the houses we'll go to the Council Chambers and we'll say, 'We've come again, we've built the houses and now your ragged-arsed sons have come to build you your cities.'

YOUNG STONEY: With their ragged arses!

YOUNG JESSIE: And shall us be proud?

YOUNG ANDY [*as they now move off in triumph*]: Aye, us'll be proud, they'll be proud. 'Build us cities,' they'll say, they'll command. 'Build us cities of light.'

SCENE THIRTEEN

A Town Hall chamber.
It is the year 1947.
ANDY *and* CHAIRMAN *of local town planning.*

CHAIRMAN: We're not interested, we can't be interested. You must be mad to imagine my committee would ever have given it a thought. New cities? New ones? When we've made promises about post-war slum clearances?

ANDY: Slum clearances? Patchwork! All over the country bits and pieces of patchwork. I've done it.

CHAIRMAN: Rooms, give 'em that – to eat and sleep, give 'em that. Four walls, to keep out wind and rain – that's what we promised and that's what we'll give 'em.

ANDY: Patchwork, patchwork.

CHAIRMAN: People owning all their own houses? Workers owning their own factories? This Labour Council wouldn't last five minutes if we proposed a lunatic scheme like that.

ANDY: You sold us different dreams while we were at war, mister.

CHAIRMAN: Yes, yes, dreams – I know all about the spirit of 1945. Some intellectual loud-mouth does a bit of dreaming during wartime and we're left to give it shape and practice in peacetime.

ANDY: And what a botch you make of it.

CHAIRMAN: Don't be cheeky wi' me, Cobham. You're a respected man now, a famous architect, a war hero and all that, but don't battle me with your insults. I've been in the game too long –

ANDY: Aye, and don't you talk like it, too.

CHAIRMAN: I'm twice your age and I've been a bloody founder of this local Labour Party, a founder –

ANDY: – and you act like you're the only ones can inherit the good bloody earth! You think you've got the prerogative on suffering, don't you? I can see you all, spending your time boasting who was out of work longest in the good old days. Your lot wear your past so bloody smugly, my God —

CHAIRMAN: Right now, lad, be easy. You mustn't think because I'm firm that I don't see —

ANDY: I mean, what's the difference? What's the bloody difference? The opposition used to give the same sort of answer — only they offered round the drinks meanwhile.

CHAIRMAN: Oh, lad, I'm sorry, here, I'm sorry, of course, what'll you have?

ANDY: My! Look how you rush to copy them.

CHAIRMAN: Now listen to me, Mr Cobham —

ANDY: Why not offer me tea, a good cup of strong working-class tea.

CHAIRMAN: Well tea then, tea, lad — MAISY! Two teas, luv!

ANDY: Now why should you offer me tea? That's why you and your puritanical colleagues will never do this city proud, you're such cheapskates. Give me a whisky, Mr Comrade Chairman Jackson, I'm worth it. You get used to the idea that it's worth paying for what it's worth paying for! MAISY, we don't want any teas! A good whisky, a double one, 'cos you'll go a long way to find an architect like me in this city.

CHAIRMAN: Not in all my years have I been so —

ANDY: Socialist? Socialist Council, you call yourself?

CHAIRMAN: MR COBHAM —

ANDY: Don't stop me, I'm in full flight. Socialist! 'Four walls, Mr Cobham, to keep out wind and rain, just somewhere to eat and sleep, Mr Cobham.' Practical men? I spit 'em! Facts, Mr Jackson: when I told this council years ago that Floral Houses should come down or they'd fall down, the reply was 'Nonsense! We've got schools to build, can't afford it.' Well, they fell and the new school was missing ten children. Facts: the last Labour Housing Chairman approved designs for houses that now let in so much water half the inhabitants are in sanatoriums suffering from TB. And you, even you built a block of flats on top of an underground river. You practical boys are so mean-spirited that in half a century you'll turn us into one great sprawling slum. Even your whisky's cheap.

CHAIRMAN: You're asking us to change our whole society for God's sake.

ANDY: Hallelujah!

[*Pause.*]

CHAIRMAN: You're married, aren't you, Cobham?

ANDY: Aye.

CHAIRMAN: How many children?

ANDY: Three.

CHAIRMAN: Insured?

ANDY: Eh?

CHAIRMAN: Is everyone insured?

ANDY: Insured? What are you on about, insured? I'm talking about a new kind of city and all he can talk about is insurance.

CHAIRMAN: I'm not a fool, Cobham, and you listen, you listen, you listen to me. Patchwork? Slum clearance – patchwork? Right. I agree. And what's more I agree for your reasons: the intrusion of a little bit of order in the midst of chaos. Useless. I agree. Patchwork. I agree. Because one day the chaos will overwhelm the tiny bit of order, won't it? Very clever. You know it, you're not a fool. A bit romantic, maybe, but so what, a good quality, a fault on the right side as they say.

But think, think, Cobham, your cities, those beginnings of the good life. Think. You've not let us fool you, so you won't fool yourself, surely? *You* know why the cities won't work – them's also patchwork. Them's also a little bit of order in the midst of chaos. Bits of oasis in the desert that the sun dries up, that's all. Do you like my poetry? I can spin the right phrase out when I try, you know. I can toss a metaphor or two when I want. You lads don't have the prerogative on passion, Cobham, no more than we've the prerogative on suffering.

Now them's thoughts for you, them's real thoughts for you, you think on 'em.

[*Pause.*]

ANDY: Whether you stonewall, whether you legislate, whether you lobby, argue, deceive or apply your lovely reasonable sanity, the end is the same. A cheapskate dreariness, a dull caution that kills the spirit of all movements and betrays us all – from plumber to poet. Not even the gods forgive that.

[*Curtain.*]

ACT TWO

SCENE ONE

As curtain rises we hear the words of ANDY *from previous scene 'Whether you stonewall . . . Not even the Gods forgive that.'*
The riverside some days later.
ANDY *and* KATE. *She is sewing hem of old coat.*

KATE: And when you told him that not even the gods will forgive him what did he say?

ANDY: He'd take the risk.

KATE: And so?

ANDY: And so – nothing!

KATE: Nothing?

ANDY [*angrily picking up stones to throw skimming over water*]: Slum clearances, that's what I'll do. Patch it up. Crutches, give 'em crutches.

KATE: How easily you've inherited the language of your critics.

ANDY: Well what do you expect? '*They'll* command us,' we used to say. '*They'll* command *us!* Look at us, what betrayed ragged-arses we are; weaned on passion. Poor old passion! Poor, bloody, old passion! And for what?
[*Pause.* KATE *stops sewing.*]

KATE: Andy, you want to do it alone don't you?

ANDY: Are you mad?

KATE: Andy, why don't you do it alone?

ANDY: The odds are too great.

KATE: That's no reason.

ANDY: I'm too old.

KATE: That's no reason.

ANDY: Too tired, too wise.

KATE: No reason, no reason at all. Now, let's begin again. Andy, why don't you do it alone?
[*He refuses to answer. She starts sewing again.*]

Yes, well perhaps you're right. The idea of a Golden City is dreary anyway.

ANDY: I must have been mad.

KATE: Who ever believes a call to arms?

ANDY: Don't tempt me. It's just too easy to tempt me.

KATE: Who ever heard of enthusiasm commanding attention?

ANDY: I tempt myself all the time.

KATE: There's something so much more significant about despair, isn't there?

ANDY: I'm just the sort of fool to be tempted.

KATE: You could always say you tried, very honourable; all the glory of good intentions without the actual struggle.

ANDY: You're becoming a nagger and that's what I'd become if I did it alone, a righteous old nagger.

KATE: All right, Andy, I'm going home.

ANDY: Going? Don't I amuse you?

KATE: Perhaps you'd like to stand on your head for me?

ANDY: Aye, that if you like.

KATE [exploding]: Andy, I'm tired of timid lads who laugh at themselves. I'm tired of little men and vain gestures. I have a need, O God how I have a need to see someone who's not intimidated. Who's not afraid to be heroic again.

ANDY: Kate, the hero is a bore.

KATE: As you wish. [Makes to leave.]

ANDY: The hero is a sign, you old nag you – a sign of failure.

KATE: Ah! Failure, that's what you're afraid of?

ANDY: Yes, of course I'm afraid of failure – petrified. A golden city is doomed to failure, don't you understand? One city, six cities, a dozen – what difference? It's all patchwork – like the chairman said. There'd be plenty wanting to help me patch up – oh, yes – and then when it was done they'd heave a sigh of relief that they'd managed to stave off the real revolution for yet another century. Why shouldn't I be afraid?

KATE: Then I ask you, since the bloody revolution you would like cannot be achieved – what is there left worth doing?

[Pause.]

ANDY: Who would build the city with me?

KATE: Your friends – where are they?

ANDY: Stoney, Paul? The war lost us. It would be like digging up the dead.

KATE: Then do that, wake the dead.

ANDY: I haven't the language of heroism, Kate.

KATE: Then forge it.

ANDY: From what? The words of politicians?

KATE: Forge it.

ANDY: From the old poets?

KATE: Forge it.

ANDY: From the pages of dead pamphlets?

KATE: Forge it, forge it.

ANDY: The language of heroism is a dead language, Kate. You need to be desperate to forge it.

KATE: A desperate language? Forge it.

ANDY: A desperate language breeds desperate deeds for God's sake.

KATE: Then I ask you again – what else is there left worth doing?

[*Long pause. The revolve slowly brings on next scene. They 'walk'.*]

ANDY: You know, recently I attended a May Day demonstration – a dreary march, from one street corner to another. *There* were the usual half-hearted banners and *there* were the isolated hand-claps from the handful of people on the pavements; and in front of the march, sure enough, there was our foremost political leader of the left, giving his uncertain smiles and nods to empty streets and embarrassed children. And when the marchers arrived at their destination this foremost political leader of the left stood up and made a speech about pensions and housing and the balance of trade. And suddenly, out of the crowd, a young lad shouted, 'Inspire us!' Now, think of him, Kate. My God, inspire us.

SCENE TWO

ANDY's *study, some weeks later.*

PAUL, STONEY *sit in uneasy silence.* KATE *sits, watching their reactions.*

PAUL: Well, inspire us then.

ANDY: I see, you're going to make it difficult, are you?

PAUL: Why not? You've dragged us from the peace of our homes, now pay for it.

STONEY: You've become aggressive, Paul. It doesn't suit you.

PAUL: And you've become senile. I've no patience with people who still think they can advance human progress.

KATE: That's a dreary piece of cynicism. Is that the level of your disillusionment?

STONEY: I don't suppose Andy expected the joy of an old comrades' reunion – did you, Andy?

ANDY: Now that you're here I'm not sure what I expected.

PAUL: Well, you'd better hurry up and find out, hadn't you?

STONEY: We're not being gracious, I'm feeling.

[*Awkward silence.*]

ANDY: Look at you both! You'd love to help me build these cities but you're too mean to show it. Look at you! Shrinking your poor little souls behind those comfortable disenchantments. How you wail and you whimper and you whine. [*Mocking.*] 'I've no patience with people who still think they can advance human progress.'

[*Pause.*]

PAUL [*reluctantly*]: How much will it cost?

ANDY [*jumping to it. He's got them.*]: Good! A city for a hundred thousand inhabitants would take fifteen years to complete and cost £156,000,000.

STONEY: £156,000,000?

ANDY: That means every man must find £1,560 for everyone in his family – to pay not merely for their houses but for all the public buildings as well.

STONEY: You've been working hard.

ANDY: I've got a questionnaire here, I've worked one out, we'll ask each person what kind of city he wants. Participation! We'll involve them, a real community project, a real one!

STONEY: And *our* roles? [KATE *impatiently rises to pour drinks.*] Each of us here? The part we play, tell us those. We're a bit of a battered lot, us. Look at us.

PAUL: What must we do now? Search our souls for some sort of credentials?

STONEY: Aye, in a way, credentials – a sort of worthiness.

KATE: The reverend Dean wants to know if we're good people, don't you, dear?

STONEY: Yes, I do – is that wrong?

KATE: So look at us, Andy. What do you see? [*Giving* PAUL *his drink*.] A good journalist who might have made a good poet but didn't. Partner number one – frustrated! Terrible credentials. Go home, Paul Dobson. A minister, a religious administrator, a lover of love who can't bring himself to admit how dulled he is by his experience of it – partner number two. Terrible, terrible credentials – back to your desk, Reverend Jackson. And finally myself, daughter of impoverished aristocracy, a woman with a constant sneer in her voice, unloved and with no respect for the will of the people. Why don't we all go home, Reverend Jackson?

[*Silence.*]

STONEY: Where is Jessie, Andy?

KATE: Oh, my God!

STONEY: Why isn't she with us? She was part of us, once. Why does she stay in the kitchen?

KATE [*impatiently*]: Yes, where is your housekeeper? Why isn't your housekeeper asked to contribute to the discussions?

STONEY: See what I mean, Andy? She could never build such a city as you want, never! If I were Andy I'd have slapped the arse off you for that, but good and hard.

ANDY: Ignore it, Stoney. We don't have to be saints to have dreams.

STONEY: I cannot build your city with the sneers of a dying aristocracy ringing in my ears.

KATE: I'm not a dying aristocracy – I'm classless.

STONEY: Classless? The common man would smell you decaying a mile off.

KATE: The common man! What a fraudulent myth – the glorious age of the common man! My God, this is an age of flabbiness, isn't it? You know, Stoney, it's not really the age of the common man, it's the age of the man who is common, and if it's unforgivable that my class has produced the myth, then you should weep, yes weep, that your class has accepted it.

Haven't you noticed how we pat you on the head at the mere sign of intelligence? 'He reads,' we say; 'how quaint, give him newspapers with large print', but we keep the leather-bound volumes of poets on our shelves. Haven't you noticed the patronizing way we say, 'He's artistic, how touching – give him pottery classes and amateur theatricals' – but the masters continue

to hang on our walls and the big theatres are our habitat, not
yours.

ANDY [*mocking*]: 'Our homes are made of brick with crisp square
lines and fully equipped kitchens.'

KATE: — but ours are the Georgian mansions out in the fields and we
have rooms for our guests while you, you have just enough for
your family.

PAUL [*catching on*]: 'We're well fed and there's ample roast beef at
home.'

KATE: — yes, Paul. But we know the taste of caviare, don't we? And
there are vintage wines on our tables.

STONEY [*also catching on*]: 'And in this day of the man who is
common and drives his Austin and Ford we think we're equal to
any man.'

KATE: — but we have the Bentley and the Rolls and keep quiet.
[*Pause.*]

STONEY: So?

KATE: So, because we need to perpetuate the myth that class differ-
ences are past, we pat his head and consult the man who is common
in the name of the common man. Questionnaires, Andy? [*Holding
one up.*] Is this what you imagine makes it the age of the common man? This? [*Reading.*] 'For the people who plan to inhabit
the new cities so that we may know better how to build them.'
Fancy! Architects asking laymen how to build a city. Why
should the man who buys his city know how to build it? Why
shouldn't we turn to you for our homes, to the poet for his words,
to the Church for its guidance? Participation? It's a sop, dear,
to ease your conscience. Tear them up — be brave, you know
well enough how you want those cities built — shall we tear them
up?

[ANDY *pauses, uncertain. Then he takes questionnaire and tears it
up.*]

PAUL: But Andy's not even convinced himself. It's all patchwork, he
says. How can he persuade others of a glory he doesn't believe in
himself?

ANDY: If I decide to build those cities, then I'll forget they could
ever have been regarded as patchwork, I'll ignore history.

PAUL: And what makes you think we'd ever agree to this massive
piece of self-deception?

ANDY: Paul, if I'd come to you with brave declarations and the cry of an easy Utopia would you have believed that?

[*Pause.*]

PAUL: No, I'd not have believed that.

ANDY: Then what else is there left worth doing? The alternative is that complete revolution we all used to talk about, but today? Here? Now? – there's no situation that's revolutionary, is there? Face it, all of you. There – is – no – revolutionary – situation.

[ANDY *challenges them all but there is only silence.*]

Then let's begin.

In the way you build a city you build the habits of a way of life in that city – that's a fact. Six Golden Cities could lay the foundations of a new way of life for all society – that's a half-truth, one that we're going to perpetrate, with our fingers crossed.

STONEY: And the method?

ANDY [*with fresh energy. Now he's really captured their interests*]: Simple. There are architects and town planners throughout the country who I know would form six working committees to find sites and draw up plans.

PAUL: And the initial cost?

ANDY: Each committee would need £5,000 to open up offices for the first year. A year of planning, building models, battling authorities and finding the first 16,000 inhabitants. I've already set aside £5,000 for our first offices.

STONEY: And the inhabitants? How do you begin to look for them?

ANDY: When the whole scheme is announced in the press there'll be thousands of applications – I know it. We'll invite the applicants to attend a Monday Meeting which we'll conduct weekly for perhaps the first five years – maybe more. And at these meetings the plans will be explained in detail and we can select the right age groups and create the correct balance of professions.

PAUL: And the money? How will the first money come in?

ANDY: Instalments. Before the work can begin, each family will have to start paying instalments on their house – no, their city! It'll take three years to accumulate sufficient capital to start building.

STONEY: And how long will it take before they can move in?

ANDY: Five years, five years for the first phase of building.

STONEY: Five years? Three years to start and five years of building?

Eight years, Andy. You're asking people to wait eight years to move into a house.

PAUL: Don't be so dull-witted, Stoney. They'll be waiting eight years for their own city, more than their own house.

STONEY: It's paralysing.

PAUL: One last question – industry. The money for industry – who'll provide that?

ANDY: Industry. Aye, well, there lies the major battle.

[*The* YOUNGSTERS *wander in. They will group themselves around the catafalque to listen to a story from* YOUNG ANDY. *Firstly, though,* OLD ANDY *begins telling it. Then* YOUNG ANDY *echoes him.*]

Now, be patient, and I'll tell thee a story. There was a man called Joseph Arch, once ...

SCENE THREE

The Cathedral.

PAUL *and* STONEY *are lying around in resting positions, listening to the story* ANDY *is telling* JESSIE.

ANDY: There was a man called Joseph Arch once, a farm labourer from Warwickshire, born about 1850. And one day three men called on him, in his house, and asked him to be their leader. They wanted him to come that night into a town called Wellingbourne; there was to be a meeting. They wanted, they told him, to get the local farm labourers together and start a union directly. 'Oh,' he said, 'a union, is it? You'll have to fight hard for it and suffer for it,' he said, 'you and your families,' he said. They told him they knew that and they and their families were ready.

JESSIE: Did it succeed?

ANDY: No, it was smashed – but they'd begun, and once the Combination Laws were repealed they stopped going underground and started in earnest.

Now,

consider, it's only about sixty years later, just that, a lifetime only, and look – there's all those people, all that organization, all those improvements. Now that strikes me as an exciting story but no one seems to have seen what happened. They know wages have gone up, they can see improved housing and better working conditions, but no one seems to have seen much else. It's like, it's like – how should I tell you? – it's like some people who are stranded on an island and a hundred miles away is the mainland, so they must build a boat. Now they only want the boat to carry them for a little way, for a short time; but as they build it they sink holds and erect decks, they build cabins and kitchens, they give it a polish and lots of sails and all they do is travel a hundred miles from one piece of land to another. But that's daft, isn't it? I mean, why don't they seem to realize they could live on it, trade in it, travel right across the world in it? 'No,' they say, 'we only wanted it to go from the island to the mainland – that was its only job.' So there it is, in the harbour, and they keep it polished, waiting for another emergency – but that's all.

And I don't know –

but it seems to me that someone has to tell them that that ship can span every ocean there is, every ocean, look, and reach all corners of the world. It seems to me – someone has to tell them that . . .

[*Now* OLD ANDY *is being revolved on. The* YOUNGSTERS *remain.* YOUNG ANDY *continues with his story.* OLD ANDY *echoes him.*]

SCENE FOUR

The Trades Union Congress. It is the year 1948.
A back projection of the General Council who are listening to ANDY *addressing Congress.*
ANDY *is alone on a rostrum.*
A long cloth banner stretches behind him with the words ANNUAL TRADES UNION CONGRESS.
At the base of the platform of the General Council is a decoration of flowers.
Note: He must *not* address the next speech to the audience.

YOUNG ANDY echoed by ANDY: Someone has to say, 'Look, look at that ship, it's more than a raft, it has sails. The wind can catch those sails and the ship can span every ocean there is. It can span every ocean and reach all corners of the earth.'

ANDY [*continuing alone*]: Why did we build such a ship, with eight million people aboard? To raise our wages every year by pennies? To ensure that our offices are guarded by first-aid kits and our factories have posh flush lavatories? Is that all? When with the lovely voice of all our energies we could command the building of the most beautiful cities in the world. More – the most beautiful world itself, I tell you.

Years ago, many years ago, when I first came into the movement, at a time of scant employment, falling membership and apathy – a man asked a question. Some of you will remember that man – Jake Latham, chairman then, dead now. The movement had been alive for half a century, half a hundred years of argument, and achievement, look; yet – the 1933 crisis came and apathy confronted him. 'What,' he asked, he was an old bewildered man, 'what, since we have failed, is there that holds men in a movement through all time? Any movement, not even a movement – groups, a family, a community, a civilization?' He had no answer. Tired – he was a tired, old man.

But is this us? Old men? Tired old men? The most terrible war in history is won – by us –. we should be jubilant, we should be singing. We should have answers and not be doubled up by despair. Old men have no answers and when old age is ours, then, then we can cry in bewilderment. But now, our blood is young, we should cry – we know! Old age laments, leave lamentations till the grave – *we* know! *We* know what holds men in a movement through all time – their visions. Visions, visions, visions! What else? To fight for a penny more an hour for standing at the lathe, our energies for only this? A movement built for only this? The battle for our daily needs?

But men have minds which some good God has given so we can tackle problems bigger than our daily needs, so we can dream. Who dares to tell us we've no right to dream? The dull and dreary men? Then tell the dull and dreary men to crawl away.

I tell you,

this resolution now before you builds a dream. In the way you shape a city you shape the habit of a way of life.

I tell you,

we have a city we can build, we *have* a city. We have a city we can build out of whose contours comes the breath of such a brave new world.

[ANDY *is revolved off. The first Monday Meeting revolved on. Now it is* STONEY *who is echoing* ANDY.]

ANDY echoed by STONEY: I tell you,
the dull and dreary men preach caution, caution is a kind of fear. The dull and dreary men breed apathy, apathy is a kind of cancer. But look, *we* have a city. The dull and dreary men, beware – beware the dull and dreary men.

I tell you, look –
we have a city, we can have a city!

[*The speech ends to coincide with next set in position, and the applause of the Monday Meeting public who are also in position. The* YOUNGSTERS *move off to continue sketching.*]

SPECIAL NOTE

From here on begins the 'continuous' scene – divided into 15 parts – that is to say, a scene taking us right to the end of the play as one set dissolves rapidly into another. It will cover many years and many situations and the purpose of proposing this method of staging is to create a sense of purpose, bustle, activity and – most important – growth and decay. The long battle to build the city will begin and end in this 'continuous' scene. Towards the end of each situation (set), preparation will be going on for the next situation (set), so that characters will turn immediately from one phase of the development to another. Similar to the style up till now, only more so. It must appear as one continuous movement, slowly and inexorably unfolding – rather like watching the painting of Dorian Gray slowly change from a young man into an old and evil man – as in the film.

[*The screens will remain apart till the final scene.*]

SCENE FIVE

Covering the years 1948–85 or thereabouts.

PART ONE

The Golden City offices.
This is the first of the 'Monday Meetings'.
'Monday Meetings' will continue as the years go by, and though them we
will build up a verbal image of the cities.
A board hangs in the background:
'MONDAY MEETING – FIRST WEEK'
STONEY *has just addressed the audience.* KATE *and* PAUL *are in attendance.* KATE *is obviously angry about something.*

STONEY [*acknowledging applause*]: Thank you. Now, we'll be happy to answer questions.

QUESTIONER: Right! You've shaped the city. Very good! There are the plans, we've seen them, very good! But you want questions. Here's one. What about its spirit? The city's spirit – how will you shape that?

PAUL: Good question. A city's spirit, what will be the city's spirit? Look, look more closely at these plans. What do you see?

STONEY: Variety – that's what you see. Roads that are wide and alleys that ramble.

PAUL: Bold squares and intimate corners.

STONEY: There's colour in that city, and sound.

PAUL: And movement of line and patterns of mass.

STONEY: Not a frightening city, not intimidating.

PAUL: And its heart? What do you see as its heart? Industry may be a city's backbone but what should be a city's heart?

VOICE: A Town Hall?

STONEY: Look again – look more closely at these plans again. You can't seriously place a Town Hall at the city's heart – not a place where functionaries meet to organize our tax affairs and drainage problems.

175

PAUL: No. Our city's heart is its gardens, concert halls, theatres, swimming pools.

STONEY: Dance halls, galleries and meeting rooms.

PAUL: Restaurants and libraries, look – a rearrangement of priorities.

STONEY: And you can build it, over many years it's true, but you can build it. It's not been done before. No one's ever challenged men to pool their money and build their own city –

PAUL: – but it can be done.

[*It's the end of the meeting. The audience rise to go, murmuring, impressed.*

ANDY *enters.*

PAUL *shakes hands goodbye with one of the audience.*]

I mean, we oughtn't to be afraid . . .

KATE [*to* ANDY]: You didn't turn up.

ANDY: How many came?

KATE: You didn't turn up.

ANDY: How many came I asked.

STONEY: Twenty.

KATE: The first of the Monday Meetings and you didn't turn up.

ANDY: You couldn't have understood, Kate, Jessie was ill.

KATE: Are you going to neglect this project every time there's an upset in the family?

ANDY: You forget yourself, Kate.

KATE: Answer me. Is this project to grow depending on the ups and downs of the Cobham household? Is it?

ANDY: The woman had a miscarriage for God's sake.

KATE: So? There are doctors to guard the sick, you have other things to guard.

ANDY: Thank you but I'll make my own decisions of priority.

KATE: Your decisions, any decisions you make, affect this project. I charge you again – your family is your family and your work is your work, and you have not the right, no right at all, to neglect a project involving so many for the sake of your own good life.

STONEY: And we were the ones just talking about the good life?

KATE: Don't! Don't confuse what we preach with what we must do.

ANDY: Kate!

KATE: Yes, cry 'Kate', but I warn you – those of us who build the Golden City can never live in it, never.

[*Silence.* STONEY *and* PAUL, *embarrassed, leave.*]

ANDY: We need more funds, the kitty is low.

KATE: Nurse that then. There's the illness, find funds.

[KATE *leaves.*]

PART TWO

It is ANDY's *study.*

ANDY *opens a drawer, pulls out some drawings and tears them up.*
JESSIE *enters. Watches him a while.*]

JESSIE: What are you tearing? [*No answer.*] Don't be a fool, Andrew Cobham, what are you tearing? [*But she knows.*] Have you taken to tearing every design that your customer turns down? I thought it was the habit of architects to hold on to every last sketch.

ANDY: I can remember, when I first started on my own, I swore I would never erect a building I didn't approve of – I swore that.

JESSIE: Nor you haven't, have you?

ANDY: No, I haven't.

JESSIE: Well?

ANDY: Well, woman, you know what the cynics say – every man has his price; they must be right.

JESSIE: I always thought that cynicism didn't impress you.

ANDY: And it doesn't, but facts do and the fact is we've hardly any money left and my designs for the technical college have been turned down – too expensive.

JESSIE: Can't the project start paying you a salary now? You've been going a year –

ANDY: Now stop that. I've told you. The funds are low. The project and this household must live off the practice; that's why I built it.

JESSIE: Andrew Cobham, as the years go on it gets harder and harder to live with you. I'll not have you grunting and storming through this house because you're building a building you don't want to build. You, with a screaming and snapping head above what you are, is more than I can bear. We'll –

ANDY: A screaming and snapping head above what I am, eh?

JESSIE: It's not been a happy year that's gone, not a calm one.

[*Pause.*]

ANDY: I'll build them anything they want, Jessie. And my City is my price.

PART THREE

[JESSIE *leaves. We hear the sound of applause.* ANDY *has just addressed a Monday Meeting. Two or three from the meeting come to greet him. He chats with them as he prepares to go to the Ministry of Town and Country Planning. A doting* STONEY *helps him on with his coat.*]

ANDY: Right! We have a site. At last, after a year of searching, the first site for the first city has been found. And why? Because the number of people who've started to buy their own city has grown and everyone's started to take us seriously. They've had to: the money's coming in and that's a fact, that money is, a fact! Now – permission. One small council has offered us a site and the Ministry of Town and Country Planning must give permission to build. They must! They can't refuse! There's too much enthusiasm! Look at us – our hundredth Monday Meeting and our audiences have risen from twenty to six hundred and that's not the largest audience of applicants we've had, no! Not by a long road! Do you know this scheme has captured the imagination not only of this country but of countries throughout the world. Aye! Throughout the world! The Ministry will have to give its blessing, Tory though it is. And you know what we'll say to them? 'You'll have the finest planners in the land at work,' we'll say. 'We'll make such innovations that you'll find a dozen problems solved in one go.' They can't refuse. Look at the size this meeting was, consider the response, they can't refuse. Goodbye. Thank you.

[*They wish him luck as he moves off. We are now in a corridor in the Ministry of Town and Country Planning. An* OFFICIAL *talks to* ANDY.]

PART FOUR

OFFICIAL: Mr Cobham, it really was kind of you to come but believe me, there arrive at these offices, every day, half a dozen plans and schemes by lunatics who think they can solve our housing problems in an hour. Not that I dare imply you are a lunatic; we are all aware, even the Minister I'm sure, of your fine achievements as an architect – but Mr Cobham, I couldn't even begin to interest the Minister in such a scheme.

ANDY: But the land's no good to agriculture, it's not a beauty spot, we're not even asking you for the money. Permission – that's all, authority and a signature, at no price. We'll raise the costs, we're raising the costs –

OFFICIAL: And I don't want you to think it's because of the political implication – I know that's what you're thinking – it's not. A Ministry like this, unlike other ministries, has very little need to make political decisions, you know.

ANDY: Ah, I see, you're a classless ministry.

OFFICIAL: Yes, very aptly put, Mr Cobham, a classless ministry, yes, I like that. Good day.

ANDY: 'Yes, Mr Cobham, very aptly put, a classless ministry, I like that.'

[KATE *appears*.]

KATE: That will teach you to work through office boys. Now will you listen to me? With your reputation you're going to meet the Minister.

PART FIVE

[*A cocktail party is being prepared. A wall with a brash-coloured modern abstract 'flies in'.*

Couples are wandering on.

ALFRED HARRINGTON, *an industrialist, whose party this is, steps up to* ANDY *and* KATE. *A waiter takes their coats.*]

HARRINGTON: I can't understand why you bother with small officials. A man with your reputation should have demanded an interview with the Minister at once. Kate, why did you let this man humiliate himself, you of all people?

KATE: Give him time, Alfred – we inherited our arrogance, manipulating people comes easy to us.

HARRINGTON: She's tough is our Kate. You have a good ally, Mr Cobham. We train them well but they stray. Look at him, you think we're cynical, don't you? Not really. We recognize ability. I'd be ashamed of myself if I allowed my politics to blind me to ability. Ability coupled with guts is irresistible. I don't like all the aspects of your Golden City, but it's alive, dear boy, it's on fire. That's how I made my fortune. I was on fire. To build dams across the rivers and create the power for light seemed the most marvellous thing in the world. I built forty of them, forty of them. My own thin line of longitude, right around the globe. I was on fire, like you. You're on fire, I can see your eyes flash! And I can't resist. You'll see the Minister, I'll take you there myself. Yes! My own thin line of longitude, right round the globe.

[HARRINGTON *moves to other guests. A more ornately moulded wall with a Constable-type painting is flown in to cover other wall.*

PART SIX

It is the more luxurious setting of the Minister's cocktail party. The Minister of Town and Country Planning – REGINALD MAITLAND *– approaches* ANDY *and* KATE.]

MAITLAND: My dear Mr Cobham, it's an honour to meet you. Alfie Harrington has been speaking about your plans for ages – it's taken so long for us to meet, forgive me. Delighted, Miss Ramsay.

[*A waiter offers drinks.*]

ANDY: It's very kind of you, Minister. I'm happy our project has gone so high as your good self.

[MAITLAND, *since women are only appendages, ignores* KATE *who moves away to listen from a scathing but dignified distance.*]

MAITLAND: I know you imagine the Conservative ministries to be filled with hostile and reactionary diehards. It's a convenient image for you people on the left to hold, but the fact is we're all hard-working men, like yourself, and in order to stay in power we just have to have the country's interests at heart.

KATE: You'll see us then?

MAITLAND: But of course I shall see you; I'd be foolish, not to say rude, if I didn't make it my business to meet and listen to the nation's most able minds.

[HARRINGTON *reappears with a new drink.*]

ANDY: I'm concerned to see this city built, Minister, and since your permission is needed then I'll seek it and be grateful to receive it.

HARRINGTON: I bet your colleagues on the left won't be so grateful.

MAITLAND: The truth about the left, dear Cobham, is that it's dreary – face it – it's dull, self-righteous, puritanical, dreary. Always known what's wrong, of course; poverty, bad housing, long working hours – basic, simple criticisms. But it's taken us on the right to rectify those wrongs and a little more besides.

ANDY: Aye, under pressure, though.

MAITLAND: 'Aye,' he said. He still retains his dialect, charming, Cobham, charming. I'm delighted to have met you. Harrington?

[MAITLAND *moves off calling* HARRINGTON *to follow him.*]

KATE: He's patronizing you. You don't feel it? Well learn to feel it. Look at you, you want so much so badly that you're leaping at small favours. Raise your head and stop smiling or you'll begin to feel you've won the moment they start confiding those funny intimate stories about famous men of power.

[HARRINGTON *returns.*]

HARRINGTON: A shrewd man, that. Talks like a fool but acts with unparalleled toughness.

KATE: Of course he's shrewd, he knows we've found our first 25,000 inhabitants –

ANDY: – and deposited our first two million pounds.

KATE: There's a great deal of political gain in being benevolent to the left.

[*The party breaks up. All go off except* ANDY.

The first of the 'building-site sounds' is heard: a pneumatic drill. It comes on loudly to establish itself then fades into the background where it will remain and be added to by other building-site sounds as the play progresses. These sounds, each different and real, should pulsate rhythmically, like a musical background.]

PART SEVEN

[*Two scenes now happen together: the present interleaves with the future.*

A Cathedral scene becomes a counterpoint to a Monday Meeting scene.

STONEY *and* PAUL *join* ANDY *to address the 300th Monday Meeting.*

THE YOUNGSTERS *enter, playfully throwing a haversack from one to the other, chanting with each throw.*]

ANDY: The building has begun. Enough money has been deposited and, ladies and gentlemen, the – building – has – begun.

YOUNG ANDY: Cities of light and shade.

ANDY: The land's drained.

YOUNG JESSIE: Secret corners and wide streets.

ANDY: The huts are up.

YOUNG PAUL: Cities for lovers, that frighten no one.

[YOUNG JESSIE *sits by catafalque, exhausted.*]

ANDY: Water supplies within easy reach, road and rail communications –

YOUNG STONEY: Cosy cities, family cities.

[YOUNG STONEY *sits by catafalque, exhausted.*]

PAUL: – and a countryside that's lovely, aye, lovely, lovely. Have you ever watched a city growing, ladies and gentlemen?

YOUNG PAUL: Cities for crowds and lone wolves.

[YOUNG PAUL *sits by catafalque, exhausted.*]

PAUL: Have you ever heard the hum of men building their own city? The walls rise and the flowers blossom.

YOUNG ANDY: Cities with sound for the blind and colour for the deaf. Wheeee!

[YOUNG ANDY, *giggling, joins his exhausted and happy friends by . the catafalque.*]

ANDY: No endless rows of dreary houses but a grand design, of steeples and spires and buildings at levels that soar and fall.

STONEY: The walls rise and the flowers blossom; the rubble turns to roads.

ANDY: Sixteen hundred homes a year, ladies and gentlemen, that's our target.

PAUL: The rubble turns to roads and the dust from machinery settles . . .

ANDY: Sixteen hundred homes a year.

STONEY: . . . and the dust from machinery settles to reveal the slate and granite, the glass and cement and all the patterns men make for the pleasure of their living.

PART EIGHT

[*During these last seconds, three men take their places behind or near a desk. They are trade union leaders, members of the General Purposes Committee of the T.U.C.,* TED WORTHINGTON, BILL MATHESON, BRIAN CAMBRIDGE. *It is an office in the T.U.C. building.*
PAUL *and* STONEY *leave.* ANDY *remains.*]

MATHESON [*reading from a small notebook, jeeringly*]: '... and the dust from the machinery settles to reveal the ...' what's this? Slate? 'the slate and granite', is it?

YOUNG ANDY: So there it is, in the harbour, and they keep it polished, waiting for an emergency, this vast organization of theirs, this 'BRITISH TRADE UNION MOVEMENT'! But that's all! And I don't know, but it seems to me that someone has to tell them: that ship can span every ocean there is, *every* ocean, look, and reach all corners of the world. It seems to me someone has to tell them that, and if we do – then they'll listen.

MATHESON: 'The glass and cement and – and – all the patterns men make for the pleasure of their living.' Yes, that's it, 'all the patterns men make for the pleasure of their living.'
Yes. Pretty words. That's what I heard. I made notes, pretty words. The 300th Meeting it was, I went to listen. Pretty words you and your artist friends make.

CAMBRIDGE: All right, Bill, don't let's start off with sarcasm, we've got business to attend to.

MATHESON: Oh, I'm not being sarcastic. Andy knows me, don't you, Andy? Our unions have worked together many a time, haven't they? He knows me.

ANDY: Aye, I know you, Bill Matheson, and I know you resent me.

MATHESON: Resent you? Resent you? You're sensitive lad – too sensitive. Why should I resent you?

CAMBRIDGE: We've got business, I said; now settle.

MATHESON: Resent you? Yes, I do bloody resent you. The old chimera, the good ole Utopian Chimera rearing its irritating little head again.

ANDY: Do I have to listen to him, Brian?

CAMBRIDGE: Settle, I said.

MATHESON: There's one turns up every five years, the good old Utopian.

CAMBRIDGE: So help me, Bill, I'll turn you right out of the bloody door if you don't come to heel.

WORTHINGTON: He's a bit sloshed, is our Bill Matheson tonight, a bit over the eight.

CAMBRIDGE: Andy, I don't suppose I have to tell you why we've called you, do I, lad? The General Purposes Committee have to try and make order of these thousand and one resolutions before

183

they're placed in front of Congress and we want to discuss the resolution your Union's putting up this year.

MATHESON: For the fourth year, mark you – that's persistence, that is, you and your draughtsmen's union. You must have a good membership behind you – wish I could get my buggers to support everything I propose.

ANDY: Start proposing the right things.

CAMBRIDGE: Now cut it out, lads, for Christ's sake. You're like a couple of bitchy females. [*To* ANDY.] I don't suppose we could persuade you to drop the resolution for this year, could we?

ANDY: No, you couldn't.

CAMBRIDGE: I mean, the more times it gets voted down the more bored the delegates get. You know how the lads are at Congress time – all sorts of bloody moods.

WORTHINGTON: It's staggering what you've done, Andy, staggering; but what about the other five cities? How's them? How's their committees going?

ANDY: Not as advanced as us, they're held back, waiting to see what happens to us. But –

MATHESON: Six cities? We must be mad to even discuss it with him. Six cities and he's asking the trade unions to finance the industry in all of them. You'd bankrupt us in six months.

ANDY: Not true – and you know it. At the rate at which they'd grow, the profits of our city could finance the industry of another. We've worked that out to the last detail – you've had the facts and figures for the last two years.

WORTHINGTON: Then why don't you build one city first and let the others follow?

MATHESON: Because one isn't enough. Because he wants the bloody glory of being a great revolutionary figure, don't you know? Haven't you heard the name he's got? The silent revolutionary – that's what the papers call him, the silent revolutionary.

WORTHINGTON: Ignore it, Andy, pass it by, answer my question – why not one city first?

ANDY: Because the prospect of six cities is the prospect of a real change. One becomes an experiment and experiments are patchwork. Remember Owen?

MATHESON: Yes, we do. Owen, Robert bloody Owen. Responsible

for shattering what little trade unionism existed in those days –
half a century wasted. We remember Owen all right.

WORTHINGTON: You're a fool, Bill Matheson, no education.
You know your trouble, don't you? You really believe in
profits.

MATHESON: Right! You're dead right. I've said it in public and I'll
say it here. It's human, it's basic to the human mentality and the
sooner we acknowledge it the sooner we'll get industrial peace.
Owenites, that's what this lot is, Owenites, and they're going to
shatter us again, I'm warning you, with their six Golden bloody
Cities.

CAMBRIDGE: Don't be daft, Bill, he didn't ever seriously think he'd
see six cities in his lifetime – did you, Andy? Not seriously. I mean
that's a bit of bargaining power you've set up, isn't it? Give way on
the other five and get your way on one? A bit of market bargaining,
eh?

ANDY: Now watch it, Brian, you're patronizing me. I've had enough
of being patronized. Just state your position and don't play politics.
I'm a tough hand and I don't need softening up, just state your case.

CAMBRIDGE: You're right, Andy, you're right. You have to face so
many nitwits on this committee that I use diplomacy when it's not
needed. I should have known better, I'm sorry. I'll put it fair and
square. For the last three years the General Council have advised
Congress not to vote in favour of financing industry in the six
cities. Now I'm not saying the General Council would ever recommend Congress to finance even one city, but it's bloody certain
they can't consider six. If you want the scheme to make sense at
all, then drop the other five.

ANDY: Drop them?

WORTHINGTON: Drop them, Andy, drop them. Build one of your
cities and change the resolution accordingly. You don't stand a
snowball's chance in hell of getting Congress to vote money for six.

ANDY: Drop them?

CAMBRIDGE: Drop them?

    [*Pause.*]

ANDY: But for one?

CAMBRIDGE: But for one – I'll tell you frankly. Your project has
focused attention on the constitutions of nearly every trade union
in the country –

WORTHINGTON: – and nearly every constitution declares its fervent aim as being the final take-over of the means of production –

MATHESON: – which everyone has forgotten – thank God –

CAMBRIDGE: – until now.

ANDY: And now the General Council are embarrassed?

CAMBRIDGE: And now the General Council are embarrassed. The success you've been having has embarrassed them. They'll have to decide something.

[*Pause.*]

ANDY: Can you guarantee they'll decide to recommend the financing of industry in one city?

CAMBRIDGE: Andy lad, for Christ's sake. You know I can't guarantee a thing like that.

ANDY: I'm really being pushed to the wall, aren't I?

CAMBRIDGE: I'd say you were being given a way out. You've now got the possibility of making one city work; before, there was the possibility of nowt. Think on it.

ANDY: I'll think on it.

MATHESON: Ha! he'll think on it!

WORTHINGTON: Oh give it a rest Bill Matheson, will you? Andy, a resolution last year called for us to make an investigation into the type of housing estates that the Government and local councils are building. You're a personal friend of the Minister now, you'd be a great asset, would you sit on the committee?

MATHESON: That's it, give him another job, he's got broad shoulders, he's a bloody hero, a silent revolutionary – don't you know.

WORTHINGTON: Take him home Brian, for Christ's sake.

CAMBRIDGE: Come on, Bill, you're like an old grandmother these days, have another drink, put you out of everybody's way.

[MATHESON *and* CAMBRIDGE *leave.* WORTHINGTON *is half-way out as* PAUL, KATE, STONEY *loom in like presiding judges. It is the Golden city office.*]

PART NINE

WORTHINGTON: By the way, lad, have you ever stopped to consider what'll happen if industry couldn't be set up in the way you want it? You'd have six cities built and an army of unemployed smouldering in them. Think on it! [*Exits.*]

[ANDY *has his back to his three comrades.*]

KATE: So, they offered you the glory of another fact-finding committee, did they? Asked you to compromise with one voice and told you they loved and needed you with another. Clever. Clever boys. What was your answer? [*No reply.*] Andy, what was your answer? [*No reply.*]

PAUL: What did you tell them, Andy?

STONEY: You didn't agree?

KATE: Leave him answer.

PAUL: Andy, you didn't agree, did you?

KATE: Leave him answer, I say.

STONEY: But he couldn't agree. There's five other committees, they've got sites, all that work, those architects, all that money invested –

PAUL: They didn't promise to finance even one city.

STONEY: Haven't we compromised enough, Andy?

PAUL: Or shall we compromise even on our self-deception?

[ANDY *turns to them.*]

STONEY: My God, how old you look just now.

ANDY: How old we all look. We'll be very old soon, boys.

KATE: Andrew Cobham, when Brian Cambridge asked you to drop the five Golden Cities, what did you say?

[*Pause.*]

ANDY [*defiantly*]: I said – aye.

[*The building-site sounds rise. The ominous thumping of the petrol-driven rammer is added to the drilling.* PAUL *walks to a part of the office where there are six rolled-up plans. He takes two and tears them in half and leaves.* STONEY *does the same with three others and also goes.* YOUNG PAUL *and* STONEY *wander off, wrapped in their own discussions.* ANDY *withdraws the last plan from the basket and unfolds it. The sounds fade low. Now* YOUNG ANDY *takes his* YOUNG JESSIE *off in another direction.* YOUNG PAUL's *tone is happily confident;* OLD ANDY's *is melancholic.*]

YOUNG ANDY echoed by ANDY: It'll be a beautiful city. They'll own their houses, work in their factories and there'll be time for all that lovely living. It'll be a beautiful city.

[*The youngsters have gone.* ANDY *hands the last roll to* KATE. *He moves to kiss her face. She turns away. He sadly leaves her.* KATE *glances dejectedly at the plan. She sits. Utterly spent. Almost near tears.*]

KATE: It'll be a beautiful city.

Have you ever watched a city growing, ladies and gentlemen? Have you ever heard the hum of men building their golden city? The walls rise and the flowers blossom; the rubble turns to roads and the dust from machinery settles to reveal the slate and the granite, the glass and cement, and all the patterns men make for the pleasure of their living.

[MAITLAND *enters*.]

MAITLAND: ... and all the patterns men make for the pleasure of their living. You all make lovely sounds when you talk about your city, lovely sounds. Why have you called me, Kate?

KATE: You know why.

MAITLAND: Are you snapping at me, Kate Ramsay? I know it's favours and help you want but I've been friend to you all for long enough now not to be resented.

KATE: You must speak to Andy again. Offer to bring industry to the city.

MAITLAND: Have the unions turned down the resolution?

KATE: The unions, the unions! The unions would have to empty half their coffers for such an enterprise.

MAITLAND: He won't bless you for urging this compromise.

KATE: Compromise? What compromise? That the workers won't own the factory they work in? As if it makes much difference whether they own the machine or not, they'll still hate it. Do you really imagine I ever believed such things would make a city golden? It'll be beautiful – enough! There'll be no city like it in the world. They'll come from the four corners – it'll be beautiful and that will be enough.

MAITLAND: When will they decide?

KATE: Congress will vote in four months' time. Andy still thinks they'll vote in favour after ten years – I know they won't. His 'life-long' boys! He's become so obstinate he can't find the strength to be honest.

MAITLAND: He won't listen to me, Kate; secretly he's always been suspicious of a right-wing Minister like me being around.

KATE: No, he's honest about you. He used to say, 'Old Maitland's earning a place in posterity, he wants to buy a piece of heaven and God's good will, and the Golden City will earn him a pass straight through the pearly gates.'

MAITLAND: Now he says?

KATE: 'Why shouldn't he buy his piece of heaven?' That's what he says now. 'Let him buy his pass, I've tried to buy mine.'

MAITLAND: I'll talk to him. After all, Kate, the city grows, the people in the city own their houses, the spirit of the place belongs to them and the co-ops have taken over most of the commerce. That's good, isn't it? He can't complain about that. But you're right. He needs heavy industry and only my 'lifelong' boys can provide that. He's got no alternative. Only you know, Kate, I can't do it alone; I can bring *some* money to the place but other people like Harrington will have to be involved.

KATE: Involve them.

[*She leaves, defiantly,* MAITLAND *following.*]

MAITLAND: I can't say I shall look forward to speaking to him. He'll snap. He snaps all the time. You all snap – been at it too long, Kate. All of you, a whole lifetime. He'll snap.

[*Building-site sounds rise. Add the shovelling of gravel.* JESSIE *appears to polish some furniture. She is older and weary. Everyone is older and weary.*]

PART TEN

[*We are in* ANDY'*s study. Sounds fade low.*]

ANDY [*off*]: Nothing! I can find nothing in this house. A mess, it's all a great sprawling mess.

[ANDY *enters. He wears a dressing-gown and he coughs.*]

JESSIE: Screaming? Still screaming, Andrew Cobham. Do you want to stay in your sick-bed longer?

ANDY: I can't have Maitland come here and see me in a dressing-gown – that jacket should have come back from the cleaners weeks ago, weeks.

JESSIE: Reggie Maitland is a Minister of Housing, he's a ruler, a man of power – he doesn't care. Now, sit in your chair, and I'll pour you a drink.

ANDY: You babble and fuss like an old washerwoman.

JESSIE: Do you want it neat or with soda?

ANDY: You *are* an old washerwoman.

JESSIE: I'll give you soda.

ANDY: And it's no good telling you. I tell you once, I tell you a dozen times, and still there's never a thing when I want it.

JESSIE: Heard from the office? How does the city grow?

ANDY: It grows.

JESSIE: What stage are you at?

ANDY: Stage? What would you know about a building stage?

JESSIE: You never talk, I have to squeeze words out of you. What stage are you at, I asked?

ANDY: Ten years have passed, it's two-thirds done – that stage.

JESSIE: Have all the people settled? They happy?

ANDY: Happy? Who knows? You can't leave misery behind, it comes with you. Ask their grandchildren.

JESSIE: And Paul and Stoney? Why do they stay away from here?

ANDY: They're tired. They work and they're tired. It's all routine now, they have private lives.

JESSIE: There was a time when your work kept you all together.

ANDY: You babble. You go on and on and you babble.

JESSIE: Friendship is a beautiful thing, you once said; people who share your – I'm sorry, I disturb you, don't I?

ANDY: Yes, you do.

JESSIE: I'm not much of a help to you, am I?

ANDY: Help? Help? You've mothered my children, you've kept my house, you cook, you mend – what other help can you give?

JESSIE: We don't even share walks to the smelly these days –

ANDY: Share, share! Everybody wants to share, everyone wants a bit of your peace or your love. Share? You share my bed.

JESSIE [*exploding*]: You've no right, Andy, you've no right. I can't add to your work, all right, I can see this, you point these things out, you keep on and on pointing these things out, but you've no right to torment me.

I'm a good mother, you say, I cook, I mend, I even iron your shirts to your satisfaction, but – words, I can never find words.

I'm not a fool; I've been made to feel it often enough, but I'm not a fool, even though I think you're right all the time, and – oh, if only I had the powers to argue and work it out – there's a wrong somewhere.

You said find your rightful place, I've found it. You said accept your limitations, I've accepted them – people should be happy with their limitations, you said. Happy! Me, happy! My only reward is to be treated like a hired housekeeper instead of your wife.

ANDY [*softer*]: You babble, you babble, Jessie.

JESSIE: Don't you know what I'm saying? Don't you hear what I'm telling? I don't mind being inferior but I can't bear being made to feel inferior. I know I'm only a housekeeper but I can't bear being treated like one.

Wasn't it you wanted to treat everyone like an aristocrat? Well, what about me? I don't claim it as a wife, forget I'm your wife, but a human being. I claim it, as a human being. [*Pause.*] Claim? I'm too old to stake claims, aren't I? Like wanting to be beautiful, or enthusiastic or in love with yourself.

    [*A pained, pained silence.*]

    The city grows, you say?

ANDY: It grows.

JESSIE: And you're satisfied?

ANDY: Satisfied?

JESSIE: I shouldn't disturb you – rest.

    [JESSIE *leaves.*
    Sounds rise slightly.
    ANDY *sits alone a while.* MAITLAND *enters. Sounds fade low.*]

MAITLAND: Andy, Andy – you're better then, good man, splendid. But you look morbid. You morbid?

ANDY: Morbid? I don't know. I just clench my teeth more, that's all.

MAITLAND: Holiday, take a holiday. I'll send you to a lovely spot I have in Greece. Go there, you don't know what pleasure it'd give me to offer you hospitality. Go there, Andy, go.

ANDY: I might, Reggie. I might at that.

MAITLAND: Excellent, excellent. Now then, I must be brief – I hate being brief, stupid life, never pausing for friendship; not even for a sickbed, stupid life. Still, let me explain. Kate's told me, the unions won't play, will they?

ANDY: There's not been a decision.

MAITLAND: I know, Andy, I know, but expectations, you must think ahead; what if they don't? They've turned it down nine times, what if they don't?

ANDY: There's not been a decision. Kate had no right. They're my boys, they're my lifelong boys and they won't let me down.

MAITLAND: Andy, Andy. I want to see that city finished, you know. I've helped it along and I want to see that city complete.

ANDY: They-won't-let-me-down!

MAITLAND: I've got a proposition – I've come to offer help. Harrington can find one half of the industry you need – I can find the other. Don't scowl, man, I –

ANDY: Slow they are, slow and cautious – but sound. I've waited ten years and I can wait more –

MAITLAND: Oh, no, you can't, dear boy. Another year and you'll have unemployment on your hands, you know it, Andy, why be stubborn? We'll wait for Congress this year, of course we will. Do you think I wouldn't like to see the complete experiment work? I'm not a diehard, you know this, but that city is beautiful, beautiful, we've nothing like it in the country – do you think I want to see it abandoned to ruin?

ANDY [*maudlin*]: You see, Reggie, we've been at it for so long. I'd rather see it in ruins than make that compromise. Ruins don't matter, you can build on ruins, but future generations always want to look back and know that someone was around acting on principle. I want them to look back and know about me. I know you want it finished, you're a good man, but you mustn't ask me to make that compromise, not that one.

MAITLAND: But the architecture – future generations will want to look back at that too. That's a lifetime's work, that's a poet's work.

ANDY: I couldn't face myself, you see.

MAITLAND: Go to Greece. Go to the sun. You need the sun. Go to the sun and think about it.

ANDY: There's been no decision.

MAITLAND: We'll wait for it.

ANDY: When there's been a decision, I'll think about it.

MAITLAND: We'll wait for it, we'll wait.

PART ELEVEN

[MAITLAND *leaves. Building-site sounds rise to crescendo. Add chugging of a tractor-engine.* ANDY *removes his dressing-gown to reveal a long white working-coat. The light grows and the scene becomes a magnificent abstract set of a building site.*

ANDY *stands and watches the scene change, listening to the howl of drilling, the whine of machines and the knock of hammers.*

Till now, we've built an image of the Golden City through words – now, visually, for the first time we must see and feel the magic and excitement of a city growing.

Two men in building helmets turn the pillars behind which is scaf-
folding.
Others in helmets remove the sets of the study and Monday Meeting
office and position, to the rear, a card table, four chairs and a deep,
plush chair.
Meanwhile, two others wait to receive a huge 'concrete' slab from
above. The slab is positioned. It is now a banquet table. A waiter
and liveried attendant 'begin' to lay the 'banquet' – glasses of cham-
pagne, bowls of fruit. But in to the earlier part of the scene, which is
the building site, come BRIAN CAMBRIDGE *and* TED WOR-
THINGTON. *All three stand, watch and listen. The sounds fade*
somewhat, but they still have to shout over them.]

CAMBRIDGE: It grows, lad, it grows.

ANDY: Aye, it grows.

WORTHINGTON: It's staggering what you've done, Andy, staggering.

ANDY: What's been decided?

WORTHINGTON: Not all you hoped for, Andy.

ANDY: What's been decided?

CAMBRIDGE: You didn't really expect them to vote in industry, you
   didn't really, did you? Private enterprise, let them do it, it's their
   job, not ours, Andy lad. Believe me, our own fights are enough. He
   didn't really hope for it, Ted.

ANDY: I hoped and I didn't hope – but?

CAMBRIDGE: But something happened.

WORTHINGTON: A last-minute amendment that suddenly ran like
   wildfire round all Congress.

CAMBRIDGE: True, like wildfire, great enthusiasm, round all the lads.

ANDY: It was?

CAMBRIDGE: To sponsor the last ten thousand inhabitants on your
   books.

WORTHINGTON: And more.

ANDY: More?

CAMBRIDGE: To erect a second trade union centre in the Golden City.

WORTHINGTON: You've got another building to design, Andy.

CAMBRIDGE: You'd better get working again, hadn't you, lad?

WORTHINGTON: We want a fine building, the best of them all.

CAMBRIDGE: We'll fill it with paintings.

WORTHINGTON: And sculpture.

ANDY: And flowers.

CAMBRIDGE: Aye, and flowers.

> [*Long pause. Then, limping up stage.*]

ANDY: Paul! Kate! Stoney!

CAMBRIDGE: What are you limping for, Andy?

WORTHINGTON: You hurt?

ANDY: My leg, didn't you know? I worked in the mines and one day the prop gave way and I used my leg instead, for five hours – till help came.

> [CAMBRIDGE *and* WORTHINGTON *leave, used to this eccentric.* ANDY *strides downstage taking off his white coat to reveal an evening suit beneath.*]

Paul! Kate! Stoney!

> [*Two helmeted men come in to turn back the pillars. One takes away* ANDY's *white coat. Eight* GUESTS *enter, four from each side, to the table, bringing their chairs behind which they stand. The* WAITER *brings on another, the liveried* TOASTMASTER *another.* WAITER *leaves.* TOASTMASTER *remains.*
> ANDY *calls again, like a man abandoned.*]

Kate! Stoney! Paul!

> [KATE *and* MAITLAND *enter to take their place behind their chairs.* TOASTMASTER *strikes ground three times, with his staff. On third strike the building-site sounds switch off immediately.*
> *Lights change.*]

PART TWELVE

> *It is the banqueting chamber of the Guildhall.*]

TOASTMASTER: My lords, ladies and gentlemen, prepare to receive your guest of honour.

> [ANDY *walks slowly, with bows, to his place at the head of the table. Applause.*
> *He sits.*
> *The guests sit.*
> *The* TOASTMASTER *again knocks three times.*]

My lords, ladies and gentlemen, pray silence for the Right Honourable Reginald Maitland, Her Majesty's Minister for Town and Country Planning.

> [*Applause.*]

MAITLAND: My lords, ladies and gentlemen.

For those whose minds are mean, whose sense of national pride is bankrupt, it will be considered strange that a Minister of the right should stand to pay tribute to a leader of the left. But a strong nation is not made by mean and bankrupt men; for this reason I have no hesitation in taking my place here tonight to extend, across the political barrier, a hand of sincere congratulations to one of our country's most brilliant architects. We all know his most famous and greatest achievement: for fifteen years I have watched and been proud to help, where I could, the building of the Golden City. The Labour Movement can be proud of its son and those of us in the opposition who have had to work with him know – tough and resolute though he was – that he was a man who could keep his word, abide by agreements and not allow party politics to interfere with what we all knew to be right for the nation. And this nation, this proud little nation, knows, has always known how to honour and pay tribute to such men.

My lords, ladies and gentlemen, I give you – Sir Andrew Cobham.

ALL: Sir Andrew Cobham!

[SIR ANDREW *rises.*

Applause.]

ANDY: My lords, ladies and gentlemen. I am too old now to begin explaining and excusing the indulgences I allow myself. If the country where I was born and to whom I have given my best, sees fit to honour me, then I must allow it to honour me in the only way it knows how. Having spent a lifetime bullying traditionalists in order to bring into being a revolutionary project, it seems right to stop bullying for a moment and share at least one of the traditions of my opponents.

I suppose I will soon accustom myself to answering to the name, Sir Andrew – we accustom ourself to anything in old age. No, I mustn't be flippant, I'm honoured, and I'd be churlish and ungracious not to be – yes, churlish and ungracious not to be. After all, the Golden City is built; there were compromises but it's built, a hint, if nothing else, of what might be. It would be churlish and ungracious [*he coughs*], very churlish and foolishly ungracious –

[ANDY *begins to cough violently.*

KATE *takes him by the arm away from the table. The set revolves slowly, the guests having risen to watch, anxiously.*

The card table, chairs and armchair come to rest. The guests go, the banquet table is removed.

JESSIE *appears. She and* KATE *remove* ANDY's *jacket and help him on with his dressing-gown.*
In walking from the banqueting table to the armchair, ANDY *stoops and becomes older. It is many years later. It is* ANDY's *study.*

PART THIRTEEN

Once he is seated in the chair, JESSIE *and* KATE *face each other from either side of it;* KATE *is holding his coat.* JESSIE's *gaze challenges her right; finally* KATE *hands her the coat.*]

JESSIE [*to* KATE]: You shouldn't have treated me like a hired house-keeper. You've damaged yourselves now, haven't you? Both of you, for all time.

[JESSIE *and* KATE *leave.*

ANDY: *sits a long time alone. Finally* –]

ANDY: I must stop clenching my teeth, I really must try and prevent my teeth from clenching. Howl, that's what I'd do if I opened my mouth – howl. Unclench your teeth, you old fool you. But why is it that I don't want to talk? Because I don't, you know, not a word. One day – I know it – one day I shan't even see people and then what'll happen. I shall stay just still like, petrified, because I won't be able to find a single reason why I should make one word follow another, one thought follow another.

There, look, my teeth were clenched again.

Do you know what depresses me? Men need leaders, that's what depresses me. They'll wait another twenty years and then another leader will come along and they'll build another city. That's all. Patchwork! Bits and pieces of patchwork. Six cities, twelve cities, what difference. Oases in the desert, that the sun dries up. Jake Latham, Jake Latham – ah, Jake Latham.

My lifelong boys! *My* lifelong boys? Prefects! That's all; the Labour movement provides prefects to guard other men's principles for living. Oh we negotiate for their better application, shorter working week and all that but – prefects! They need them, we supply them.

Still, nothing wrong in that I suppose; a bargain! A gentlemen's agreement, understood by everybody. They let us build the odd Golden City or two, even help us and in the end – look at me!

I don't suppose there's such a thing as democracy, really, only a democratic way of manipulating power. And equality? None of that either, only a gracious way of accepting inequality.

[JESSIE *enters. She has some 'petitpoint' in her hand.*

KATE, HARRINGTON *and* MAITLAND *also appear and take their places at the bridge table.*]

PART FOURTEEN

Look again, they were clenched again. Unclench them.

Silly old fool, you. Unclench them.

You shouldn't force people to dirty themselves. A man loves the world only when he loves himself, and what love do you have left for yourself, Andrew Cobham?

JESSIE: Talking to yourself again, Andrew Cobham. Yes, well, you always did, didn't you, old darling?

HARRINGTON: Has he been like this all evening, Jessie?

JESSIE: All evening and many evenings.

ANDY [*rising to join them at the bridge table, and whispering*]: They're good people, Jessie, all of them, you listen to me, good, good people.

[*He sits to play cards.*

JESSIE *sews.*

ANDY *deals.*]

ANDY: You know, Kate, a girl came up to me after a lecture one day and she said, 'Sir Andrew' – she spat out the 'Sir' – 'Sir Andrew,' she said, 'I don't believe you. You said all the things I believe in but I don't believe *you.*'

MAITLAND: Concentrate on the game, Andy, you're my partner now you know.

ANDY: We don't really like people, do we? We just like the idea of ourselves liking people.

KATE [*irritably*]: Play, Andy.

[*The set revolves slowly.*]

ANDY: One heart.

HARRINGTON: Double.

MAITLAND: Re-double.

KATE: No bid.

ANDY: Three hearts.

HARRINGTON: No bid.

MAITLAND: Four hearts.

KATE: No bid.
> [HARRINGTON *plays a card.*
> MAITLAND *now lays down his cards.*]

ANDY: Thank you.
> [*Music. Tallis.*
> *The screens have closed.*

PART FIFTEEN

> YOUNG ANDY *and* YOUNG JESSIE *rush into the open space and from different directions. They look at each other, shrug, and rush off again in new directions. Within seconds,* STONEY *rushes in from another direction, and off again.*
> *After another few seconds,* ANDY *slowly returns.*]

YOUNG ANDY: I am as big as it. They build cathedrals for one man. It's just big enough [*closes eyes*]. Show me love and I'll hate no one. Give me wings and I'll build you a city. Teach me to fly and I'll do beautiful deeds. Hey God! do you hear that? Beautiful deeds.
> [JESSIE *and* STONEY *rush in.*]

YOUNG JESSIE: They've locked us in.

YOUNG STONEY: Whose idea was it to explore the vaults? I knew we'd stayed there too long.

YOUNG JESSIE: They've locked us in.

YOUNG ANDY: I can't believe there's not one door open in this place.

YOUNG JESSIE: You and your stories about golden cities – they've locked us in.

YOUNG ANDY: I know there's a door open, I tell you.
> [PAUL *wanders in, pretending he's nonchalantly inspecting the ceiling.*]

YOUNG STONEY: Have you found one?

YOUNG JESSIE: Is there –?
> PAUL [*keeps them in suspense.*]

YOUNG PAUL: I've found one.

YOUNG JESSIE: He's found one, he's found one – Paul's found an open door.

YOUNG ANDY: Right, my ragged-arsed brothers – mount your horses.
> [PAUL *and* STONEY, *one arm round each other's waist, bend forward and hold on to* ANDY, *who reaches one hand back to steady* JESSIE *who has mounted on the backs of the other two. They have a chariot.*]

We knew the door was open.

YOUNG JESSIE: How did you know, my ragged-arsed brothers?

YOUNG ANDY: Because we're on the side of the angels, lass.

YOUNG JESSIE: – and are people good?

YOUNG ANDY: Aye – and people are good.

YOUNG JESSIE [*whipping them*]: Giddy up, stallions. Forward, you ragged-arsed brothers – forward!

> [*The heroic 'chariot' gallops off.*
> *Moonlight strikes through the coloured glass.*
> *Curtain.*]

END

NOTE

Old Andrew Cobham must be left on stage after the bridge scene. The last cathedral scene revolves round him as he says young Andy's lines – thus creating a dreamlike effect; the 'flash-forward' will have become 'flashback'. Old Andy must deliver Young Andy's lines wearily in contrast with the gaiety of the others, to retain the sad irony.

FOR THE BEST IN PAPERBACKS, LOOK FOR THE 🐧

In every corner of the world, on every subject under the sun, Penguin represents quality and variety – the very best in publishing today.

For complete information about books available from Penguin – including Puffins, Penguin Classics and Arkana – and how to order them, write to us at the appropriate address below. Please note that for copyright reasons the selection of books varies from country to country.

In the United Kingdom: Please write to *Dept E.P., Penguin Books Ltd, Harmondsworth, Middlesex, UB7 0DA*.

If you have any difficulty in obtaining a title, please send your order with the correct money, plus ten per cent for postage and packaging, to *PO Box No 11, West Drayton, Middlesex*

In the United States: Please write to *Dept BA, Penguin, 299 Murray Hill Parkway, East Rutherford, New Jersey 07073*

In Canada: Please write to *Penguin Books Canada Ltd, 2801 John Street, Markham, Ontario L3R 1B4*

In Australia: Please write to the *Marketing Department, Penguin Books Australia Ltd, P.O. Box 257, Ringwood, Victoria 3134*

In New Zealand: Please write to the *Marketing Department, Penguin Books (NZ) Ltd, Private Bag, Takapuna, Auckland 9*

In India: Please write to *Penguin Overseas Ltd, 706 Eros Apartments, 56 Nehru Place, New Delhi, 110019*

In the Netherlands: Please write to *Penguin Books Nederland B.V., Postbus 195, NL–1380AD Weesp*

In West Germany: Please write to *Penguin Books Ltd, Friedrichstrasse 10–12, D–6000 Frankfurt/Main 1*

In Spain: Please write to *Longman Penguin España, Calle San Nicolas 15, E–28013 Madrid*

In Italy: Please write to *Penguin Italia s.r.l., Via Como 4, I-20096 Pioltello (Milano)*

In France: Please write to *Penguin Books Ltd, 39 Rue de Montmorency, F-75003 Paris*

In Japan: Please write to *Longman Penguin Japan Co Ltd, Yamaguchi Building, 2–12–9 Kanda Jimbocho, Chiyoda-Ku, Tokyo 101*

CLASSICS OF THE TWENTIETH CENTURY

The Outsider Albert Camus

Meursault leads an apparently unremarkable bachelor life in Algiers, until his involvement in a violent incident calls into question the fundamental values of society. 'The protagonist of *The Outsider* is undoubtedly the best achieved of all the central figures of the existential novel' – *Listener*

Dark as the Grave wherein my Friend is Laid Malcolm Lowry

A Dantesque descent into hell: into Lowry's infernal landscape of Mexico – the Mexico of his masterpiece, *Under the Volcano* – and into Lowry's own personal abyss, reverberating with mental terrors and spiritual chasms.

I'm Dying Laughing Christina Stead

A dazzling novel set in the 1930s and 1940s when fashionable Hollywood Marxism was under threat from the savage repression of McCarthyism. 'The Cassandra of the modern novel in English … reading her seems like plunging into the mess of life itself' – Angela Carter

The Desert of Love François Mauriac

Two men, father and son, share a passion for the same woman – attractive, intelligent and proud, but an outcast from respectable society because of her position as a 'kept woman'. 'He writes with an intense, almost tempestuous force about the life of the emotions' – Olivia Manning

The Expelled and Other Novellas Samuel Beckett

Rich in verbal and situational humour, these four stories offer the reader a fascinating insight into Beckett's preoccupation with the helpless individual consciousness, a preoccupation which has remained constant throughout his work.

Chance Acquaintances and Julie de Carneilhan Colette

Two contrasting works in one volume. Colette's last full-length novel, *Julie de Carneilhan* was 'as close a reckoning with the elements of her second marriage as she ever allowed herself'. In *Chance Acquaintances*, Colette visits a health resort, accompanied only by her cat.

FOR THE BEST IN PAPERBACKS, LOOK FOR THE 🐧

PENGUIN INTERNATIONAL WRITERS

Titles already published or in preparation

Gamal Al-Ghitany	**Zayni Barakat**
Isabel Allende	**Eva Luna**
Wang Anyi	**Baotown**
Joseph Brodsky	**Marbles: A Play in Three Acts**
Doris Dörrie	**Love, Pain and the Whole Damn Thing**
Shusaku Endo	**Scandal**
	Wonderful Fool
Ida Fink	**A Scrap of Time**
Daniele Del Giudice	**Lines of Light**
Miklos Haraszti	**The Velvet Prison**
Ivan Klíma	**My First Loves**
	A Summer Affair
Jean Levi	**The Chinese Emperor**
Harry Mulisch	**Last Call**
Cees Nooteboom	**The Dutch Mountains**
	A Song of Truth and Semblance
Milorad Pavić	**Dictionary of the Khazars**
Luise Rinser	**Prison Journal**
A. Solzhenitsyn	**Matryona's House and Other Stories**
	One Day in the Life of Ivan Denisovich
Tatyana Tolstoya	**On the Golden Porch and Other Stories**
Elie Wiesel	**Twilight**
Zhang Xianliang	**Half of Man is Woman**

PLAYS IN PENGUIN

Edward Albee   Who's Afraid of Virginia Woolf?

Alan Ayckbourn   The Norman Conquests

Bertolt Brecht   Parables for the Theatre (The Good Woman of Setzuan/The Caucasian Chalk Circle)

Anton Chekhov   Plays (The Cherry Orchard/Three Sisters/Ivanov/The Seagull/Uncle Vanya)

Henrik Ibsen   Hedda Gabler/The Pillars of the Community/The Wild Duck

Eugène Ionesco   Absurd Drama (Rhinoceros/The Chair/The Lesson)

Ben Jonson   Three Comedies (Volpone/The Alchemist/Bartholomew Fair)

D. H. Lawrence   Three Plays (The Collier's Friday Night/The Daughter-in-Law/The Widowing of Mrs Holroyd)

Arthur Miller   Death of a Salesman

John Mortimer   A Voyage Round My Father/What Shall We Tell Caroline?/The Dock Brief

J. B. Priestley   Time and the Conways/I Have Been Here Before/An Inspector Calls/The Linden Tree

Peter Shaffer   Lettice and Lovage/Yonadab

Bernard Shaw   Plays Pleasant (Arms and the Man/Candida/The Man of Destiny/You Never Can Tell)

Sophocles   Three Theban Plays (Oedipus the King/Antigone/Oedipus at Colonus)

Arnold Wesker   Plays, Volume 1: The Wesker Trilogy (Chicken Soup with Barley/Roots/I'm Talking about Jerusalem)

Oscar Wilde   Plays (Lady Windermere's Fan/A Woman of No Importance/An Ideal Husband/The Importance of Being Earnest/Salome)

Thornton Wilder   Our Town/The Skin of Our Teeth/The Matchmaker

Tennessee Williams   Sweet Bird of Youth/A Streetcar Named Desire/The Glass Menagerie